# Maison Chance

BIỂU GHI BIÊN MỤC TRƯỚC XUẤT BẢN DO THƯ VIỆN KHTH TP.HCM THỰC HIỆN
General Sciences Library Cataloging-in-Publication Data

**Hoàng Nữ Ngọc Tim**
  Maison Chance - The Lucky House. A Future for the Less Lucky / Hoang Nu Ngoc Tim (Aline Rebeaud) ; T.P. Hồ Chí Minh: Trẻ, 2018.

  296tr.: minh họa màu ; 23 cm.
  Nguyên bản: Nhà May Mắn: Tương lai cho những số phận kém may mắn.

  1. Tổ chức từ thiện. 2. Hoạt động xã hội. 3. Lòng nhân ái.    II. Ts: Nhà May Mắn: tương lai cho những số phận kém may mắn.

  1. Charities. 2. Social action. 3. Kindness.

361.74 -- ddc 23
H678-T58

Nhà may mắn (Tiếng anh)

8 934974 156673

# Hoang Nu Ngoc Tim
## (Aline Rebeaud)

# Maison Chance

The Lucky House - A Future for the Less Lucky

TRE PUBLISHING HOUSE

# CONTENTS

Introduction................................................................8

## Part one: Maison Chance—The Lucky House

Chapter 1:    The Fateful Encounter ................................. 13

Chapter 2:    The Little Brother from the Psychiatric Center........... 23

Chapter 3:    Life and Its Side Tracks................................ 35

Chapter 4:    The Establishment of Maison Chance,
              the Lucky House at Binh Hung Hoa District ............... 41

Chapter 5:    The Birth of NGO Maison Chance ....................... 55

Chapter 6:    The Elimination of Illiteracy and the
              First Vocational Training Class........................... 71

Chapter 7:    A Second Partner..................................... 81

Chapter 8:    On the Road........................................... 87

Chapter 9:    Friends from Overseas................................. 97

Chapter 10:   Volunteers ......................................... 103

Chapter 11:   The Take Wing Center................................ 113

Chapter 12:   Between Two Places................................. 121

Chapter 13:   The Road to Independence............................ 129

Chapter 14:   A Stormy Year....................................... 143

Chapter 15:   Village Chance, The Lucky Village.................... 157

Chapter 16:   Twenty Years Went by as Fast
              as a Monsoon Downpour ............................. 173

## Part two: Real life stories

Kim Van Phuoc ........................................................................ 200

Ly Thi Bich Lien ...................................................................... 205

Nguyen Hoang Thuong ......................................................... 214

Tran Van Quang ..................................................................... 218

Ly Thi Bich Tram .................................................................... 222

Dao Minh Phung .................................................................... 225

Vo Thi Thu Hien ..................................................................... 229

Dinh Cong Duy ...................................................................... 233

Tran Tat Cuong ...................................................................... 244

Nguyen Ba Bong .................................................................... 248

Nguyen Van Lam .................................................................... 255

Ngoc Han ............................................................................... 264

Y Nam ..................................................................................... 270

Le Quyen ................................................................................ 274

Tran Quang Vuong ................................................................ 278

La Van Thanh ......................................................................... 282

## Appendices

**Appendices** ......................................................................... 287

# INTRODUCTION

Many years ago, my father suggested that I write a book on Maison Chance, whose name translates to "The Lucky House" in French. I only laughed saying, "Oh No, Papa. But thank you for the suggestion."

Later many friends also encouraged me to write as well. They promised me that it would be an easy task; I only had to write down the answers to a set of questions designed by an editorial team and they would write my book based on my answers. I declined, explaining that I had no spare time and I was also still too young to write.

Then I, myself, started thinking about writing the book. And my reasoning was that only an incredibly obstinate person would hang on to their opinion and not consider alternatives.

Who knows, the book could be a good way to spread my concept of universal love which I embrace in my heart and, if love is infectious, then thousands of readers who read my book would be infected by this love.

Finally, I accepted the inevitable. I would write the book.

I will tell you the story of Maison Chance, The Lucky House, a true story that is still going on and the end is not yet in sight.

\*\*\*

I was born in Switzerland on April 11, 1972.

My father was a journalist, and my mother was a professional singer. My little brother is deaf; I love him dearly. We learned sign language, so we could communicate with each other.

When I was ten, my mother took me to the library. She left me in the children's section to go to choose her books in the adult section. Later, she could not locate me in the children's library. She looked everywhere for me and finally found me engrossed in a large black and white photography book about Vietnam in 1951 in the Art Section.

My mother was surprised to see her daughter interested in such a strange, faraway place.

At twelve, I joined in a summer camp in Switzerland, where I met a thirteen-year-old boy named Athos. He was a very handsome boy and we liked each other a lot. After the camp ended we kept communicating by letters. My first ever boyfriend lived in an orphanage in the Italian Canton of Switzerland. Athos had no parents, he was an orphan!

At fourteen I went to another summer camp in Central Italy. Here I met Giampiero, a handsome local young man. At sixteen, he was tall and strong. He was a motor bike rider. We fell in love instantly and for the first time I held a boy in my arms. When the camp finished, I had to return to Switzerland and at the station when we parted I cried my eyes out. Then I boarded the train and Giampiero mounted his motor bike to go home. As soon as I got home I got the bad news that Giampiero had been in a traffic accident. He was seriously injured and unconscious in a hospital. Three months later he regained his consciousness, but he was only a shadow of his former self. For the whole following year, I went to Italy monthly to care for Giampiero. He had lost a lot of weight and was now a mere 66 pounds, half of his body was paralyzed, and he laid immobile, unable to make any movement. He could hardly utter a word and could not even feed himself.

The second boy I loved was a paraplegic.

At fifteen I met a much older man, a musician who lived in Switzerland, but he originally came from Vietnam. He told me stories about his birth place, introduced my taste to its delicious cuisine, and we listened to beautiful music from this country which looked on a map like the letter "S".

I was fascinated and thought to myself, "I will go to Vietnam one day."

By the time I was twenty, I had traversed North Europe and crossed the USSR, Mongolia, and China by different means of transport: trains, trucks, buses, boats, horses and even my own legs! And finally, I reached Vietnam and I've been here for over twenty years. I've shared my life with hundreds of less fortunate people: the orphans, the street kids and the disabled. We are now a cozy family known as Maison Chance, The Lucky House. In this family no one is really related to one another by blood but they all share a common experience. They were all destined to suffer a cruel fate, which could have totally destroyed them.

But their fate has taken a turn for a better future.

# Maison Chance– The Lucky House

*"Later that same night, I thought hard about the life of this abandoned boy, and about the fate of all the other helpless children without parents or close relatives to protect them! We were not all born under the lucky star, however, and this unfairness disturbed me greatly."*

# CHAPTER 1

# The Fateful Encounter

One night in early 1993 in an obscure alley in Saigon, I ran into a boy about 10 years old with dark skin. He was searching among piles of garbage and he was in a sad state: skinny, feverish and filthy.

The boy's name was Dũng and he was alone, famished and weak.

As our eyes met, I offered him my hand and we went to the noodle stall nearby. From behind her cart, the street vendor told me, "This boy is Cambodian. He's been begging around here for a few weeks."

I spoke some Vietnamese and so did Dũng. But with the help of hand signs, we managed to communicate. He explained that he came from far away, mimicking fierce soldiers carrying heavy weapons. He ate like a savage, but he got his smile back.

According to the local gossip, Dũng must have come from one of the refugee camps on the border of Cambodia and Vietnam that had been set up to accommodate the hundreds of Cambodians fleeing the Khmer Rouge. Camp conditions must have been harsh.

Sometimes entire families or groups of Cambodians escaped from the camps in the hope of a better chance in South Vietnam's biggest city, Saigon.

We stayed together for two or three hours into the night. It was late, no other Cambodians were around, and Dũng's parents had previously been murdered by Khmer Rouge soldiers. Realizing he had no relatives or shelter for the night, I took Dũng back to my hotel. I asked the receptionist permission for Dũng to spend the night in my room, but she shook her head saying, "Ah, he's the Cambodian beggar, he is dirty, and with no papers. No, he can't stay." We stood there in the hotel lobby, sad but resigned. So, we said goodbye, and the boy I wanted to help was forced to sleep in the street for another night.

Later that same night, I thought hard about the life of this abandoned boy and about the fate of all the other helpless children without parents or close relatives to protect them. They have to look for their own food and for a place on the sidewalk to rest for a few hours, always living in fear of being arrested at any time by the police. We were not all born under the lucky star, however, and this unfairness disturbed me greatly.

Next morning, I was surprised as I came out of the lobby to find the young boy waiting for me. With a big smile, I asked him to join me for breakfast. We had just met and yet we felt as if we had been friends for a long time. From that moment on I decided without hesitation that Dũng was going to be my little brother and that I would take care of him. We went to the market to buy Dũng some new clothes, soap, a pair of sandals, and also a new backpack to keep all his belongings. He was thrilled. The next thing was to get him to a friend's house for a bath; Dũng was indeed in need of a bath.

Dũng's appearance improved but he was far from well. He still had a high temperature, a persistent cough and a runny nose so I took him to see a doctor. I also took him to the dentist as he had bad teeth. Some of them had to be extracted; they were beyond repair.

The doctor prescribed a variety of medications to be taken for one week, and I religiously administered the medication right on the same street pavements where he lived still, and yet he recovered quickly.

Over the following days I spent time with my new brother. But in the evening, we had to go our separate ways and Dũng had to find his own shelter. There was a small whitewashed church nearby, built by the French colonists. In the courtyard, there was a grotto constructed of concrete with a statue of the Virgin Mary perched above. At night, the local street kids, some fifteen of them including Dũng, climbed over the church fence, which was forbidden by the law, to spend the night safely there.

Thanks to his instinct for survival, his passion for life and his pugnacity, Dũng managed to live on the sidewalks of society, dealing with all sorts of people every day, including the bad ones who stole his last dollar when he dozed off on the streets. No one cared, Dũng was alone in this giant city full of strangers who spoke a strange language which he tried very hard to learn but still he could not understand very much. So, we had something in common after all! We were both foreigners.

## Looking for a Cozy Roof

Dũng had no identification papers, so I set about getting him legal status. It wouldn't be an easy task, but I figured nothing ventured, nothing gained. I approached the Department of Labor, Returned Soldiers, and Social Services, the Foreign Affairs office, as well as any humanitarian organizations I could think of.

All were sympathetic, but none could offer any concrete help.

Dũng and I scoured the city orphanages in search of a shelter. No luck there, either. Dũng did not meet their criteria: he was neither Vietnamese nor he was young enough to be adopted out.

When at last we found a home willing to take him, Dũng refused to stay there. I remember that out of the blue Dũng put on a severe convulsive attack and began shaking uncontrollably. He acted so convincingly that everyone thought he was really mentally ill. And since this home did not have facilities to care for mentally ill patients, we were turned away once again. However, I knew he just didn't want to part from me. And the feeling was mutual!

One day, I ran into Mr. Vu, the then Director of The Youth Center Three, a government agency looking after children who had committed criminal offences. Here they applied military rules to discipline offenders and the Center was surrounded by high forbidding walls just like any other detention facility.

Mr. Vu agreed to admit Dũng and I was so relieved that Dũng had finally found a roof over his head. But I could not just leave him there on his own. I asked Mr. Vu permission to be a volunteer to the Center to teach painting and to help with the children in detention. In doing so I could not only help Dũng to integrate into the new environment but I could make my life more useful.

Mr. Vu accepted my offer, but we had to get it formalized by the Department of Labor, Returned Soldiers and Social Services before I could start working at The Youth Center Three.

That year I turned 21, but I had still not fully realized the seriousness of adopting an orphan whose birth place was at least 6,000 miles away from where I was born.

That year I was merely a young foreign girl who was not part of any international organisation. I was basically rootless in Vietnam, a country devastated by long cruel wars, a socialist country which only recently opened up to the world by reconnecting with other countries.

My visa was about to expire so I had to leave Vietnam. With no other choice, I left Dũng with Mr. Vu and boarded the bus to go to Phnom Penh, the capital of Cambodia, where I could reapply for my visa to return to Vietnam.

## In the Land of Post-Pol Pot Regime in the 1990's

The bus left from the bus terminal in Saigon's city center, a colonial building next to the famous Rex Hotel. The one-way ticket to Phnom Penh was five US dollars and the trip took from 6 a.m. till 6 p.m., a twelve-hour ride with frequent breakdowns and on bumpy red dirt roads—not to mention governmental red tape and other delays at the border.

Once on the bus, I realized that not all the young women passengers were mere tourists. They had forsaken their village life and their family to find work in the capital of Cambodia, where there was a flood of United Nations peacekeeping troops.

These girls had given up their own lives to earn some money to support their family back home. They fought among themselves over little things, hoping to find a way out of their miserable life. How tragic to see the poor Vietnamese girls selling their bodies to strange men in a strange land. Some were my age, others even younger.

We were all on the same bus, but we stopped at different stations. I was free, and they were not. Why such striking inequality? Why must each one of us be destined to different fate? Why weren't we all born under the same lucky star? The more aware I became of the scale of human suffering in this part of the world, the more I felt attached to it. It was as if I had become part of this land.

The unlucky, like Dũng, changed my life completely. Their courage and their resourcefulness helped me to understand how much they

*Dũng in front of Saigon's Huyen Sy Church*

longed and strove for a better future, a good and worthy way of life despite their lack of resources.

In April 1994, I arrived in a chaotic Cambodia only a few years after the Pol Pot's communist regime was defeated. UNTAC, The United Nations Transitional Authority in Cambodia, acted as peace keeping force during this serious time. The young soldiers came from a hundred different countries to save this country from the Pol Pot disaster. They wore immaculate uniforms and walked around aimlessly waiting for orders for action which never came. They enjoyed life as young people everywhere would; drinking beer and dancing to the music on their portable devices. They were my age, and like me, were from more peaceful societies.

Parked along the streets of Phnom Penh (which were lined with mountains of garbage often 10 yards long and which smelled unbearable) were shiny polished UNTAC jeeps with black African drivers. They were the minority among a hundred different nationalities who came here trying to solve the problem for Cambodia, a country that was being torn apart by internal strife. It was heartbreaking to see local Cambodian people all speaking the same language and yet so deeply divided that they could not peacefully coexist.

Since the international intervention, prices at the markets for food, lodging and transportation had soared. At the Phnom Penh central market, donated second-hand clothes were piled up on the ground for sale, just as they were in any other country, except that the merchandise—ski vests, Nordic winter gear, and so forth—looked out of place here, where the average temperature remained around 85 degrees Fahrenheit all year round.

There were disabled beggars on the streets, and more amputees here than in Vietnam. They had lost their limbs either in the war or they had stepped on the land mines found scattered throughout Cambodia. Most of them ended up homeless, forgotten by their families.

I also met some young children wandering the streets aimlessly like the street kids I knew in Vietnam. They were also courageous, innocent, free and happy. Their complexion was darker though.

In Cambodia, where peace was still beyond the horizon, the curfew was set before sunset. Security in the capital was maintained by men carrying heavy automatic weapons.

\*\*\*

The following morning, I went to the Vietnamese Embassy in Phnom Penh to have my visa renewed. I had been assured by the Social Services staff in Saigon that my extended visa had been faxed directly to the Vietnam Embassy in Phnom Penh so that I could return to Vietnam quickly. I was anxious to care for Dũng and to teach painting to the children at The Youth Center Three detention facility. But, strangely enough, when I turned up at the Vietnam Embassy I was informed that they had not received any instructions. I telephoned Mr. Vu and he also assured me that the Department of Labor, Return Soldiers and Social Service assured him that everything would be fine.

However, the Embassy here insisted that they had not received anything. I waited for two days before deciding to get a transit visa. I was anxious to see how Dũng was doing and to start teaching art and music at the Center.

Transit visa in hand, I boarded the bus and arrived in Saigon twelve hours later, covered with red dust. Next morning, I showed up at The Youth Center Three, only to be told that Dũng had escaped.

"On the way to the bathroom there were some washstands with a large mirror. Thành was hanging on to my arm, learning to walk step by step, when he abruptly stopped. He looked in the mirror and said to me, 'Oh, I see two of you.' I understood instantly that there were so many important things that I had to teach him."

# CHAPTER 2

# The Little Brother from the Psychiatric Center

While looking for Dũng I met many other street kids, disabled beggars and the adult homeless—all the forgotten people. Their miseries moved me beyond words and so, despite our obvious differences, I became part of their family. I took the elderly and the disabled to the hospital. I approached and pleaded with any doctors or any specialists who were willing to see them. In so doing, I met and befriended nurses and doctors who, in turn, taught me how to care for the poorest patients as well.

One hot summer day, I joined a group of young Catholics to visit a psychiatric center north of Saigon. We securely tied the boxes of prawn instant noodles to our bicycle racks then rode under the burning sun for over one and a half hours before we reached Thu Duc Psychiatric Center.

There were more than 1,500 patients of all different mental conditions at the Center. Patients were located in different pavilions, each pavilion holding 250 to 300 people, several to a room. Most patients were stark naked or just had on the bare minimum clothing. Many had scabies, a contagious skin infection causing rashes and crusty sores.

The visiting youth group began organizing games and songs in which all the patients could participate. Soon everyone was happy with big smiles on their faces, expressing a general feeling of relief and happiness for a simple reason; they were touched by our love and they felt our care through the little gifts they received.

Each pavilion had a separate unit reserved for the severely ill, with tiny cells and bars that extended to the ceiling. My heart sank as I caught a glimpse of those isolated patients sitting in their own excrement, gazing blankly into space.

*Thành and Tim at Thu Duc Psychiatric Center*

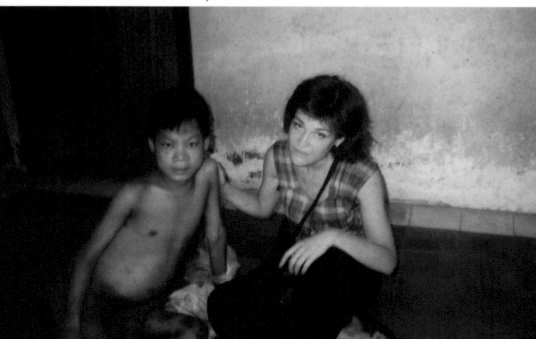

Under these disturbing conditions, I met little Thành. He had been thrown in with the adult inmates, including severely mentally ill cases. I approached his small figure and said hello. He gazed at me. His eyes were bright, but his general appearance was deplorable, nothing but skin and bones, covered in scabies from head to toe, with a pudgy face and a protruding belly. I asked if his skin itched. He nodded. Then I asked his name. "I don't know," he replied, "Nobody has called me by my name anymore."

When I enquired about Thành's health, the person in charge gave me a brutal answer in front of the boy. "He's going to die soon," and yet he was very much alive.

So, I went to the director of the unit and pressed for more information. They explained to me that Thành's chances of survival were slim. The supervisor added "In addition to his heart problems and an enlarged liver, he has fluid in his lungs and has experienced difficulty breathing." I asked permission to sponsor Thành, so I could take him to a special heart clinic. They gave me a ticket in Vietnamese: Trần văn Thành, in the care of Aline Rebeaud.

Thành was given a light green hospital uniform to wear and, thus clad, he passed through the fence that had kept him apart from the outside world for many years.

On the way to the clinic, we stopped for a meal at a roadside stall. Though still very weak, Thành ate and drank voraciously, as if it were the first time he'd tasted proper food. He also tried to smoke but his lungs rebelled, and he coughed and tossed the cigarette away.

The clinic turned out to be the most advanced cardiac institute in the country. But when the medical team heard Thành's suffocating cough they all shook their heads saying "We're sorry, Miss, but we can't do anything for him. It's too late!" I pleaded with them and always heard the same answer: "No, No, not possible. It's too late." I left the consultation room, dumbfounded by their words. I spoke to the families of other patients and they told me about another heart center, the Nguyễn Tri Phương Tim Mạch Hospital. I thanked them and hurried over there. Luckily, Thành was admitted.

## *The Race with Death*

I did not have much time to think, I was confident that my plan to leave Thành to the hospital's care overnight and come back to visit him next morning would be all right. But as I was about to walk outside, a nurse laughed and asked me: "What are you doing? You're not leaving, are you? If that's the case, you'll have to take him with you." I realized the hospital was so seriously understaffed that relatives were obliged to look after the patients.

I became his sole family. I prepared his meals, administered his medication, helped him with his personal hygiene, and most importantly, helped him to integrate into society.

Thành also suffered from arthritis. When he was in pain, I massaged him to alleviate the pain. I slept at the foot of his bed and I was there when he needed me.

Once, when Thành was still under intensive care, I fell asleep and Thành suddenly woke up. He tore off all the probes to which he was attached and got out of bed to beg food from the other patients' relatives in the ward. I had to run after him and apologized for his behavior. But people understood, they simply smiled and gave us some food.

After a month, Thành's health improved. They had pumped several bottles of fluid from his lungs and he had been given powerful antibiotics.

Thành had won the race with death.

## His Face, the Reflection of a New Life

Thành was no longer bedridden. I helped him to the bathroom, about 65 feet from the bed. Yet it was a hard and painful exercise for people suffering from arthritis, like Thành.

On the way to the bathroom there were some washstands with large mirrors. Thành was hanging on to my arms, learning to walk step by step when he abruptly stopped. He looked in one of the mirrors and said to me, "Oh, I see two of you." I understood instantly that there were many important things that I would have to teach Thành, starting with the mirrors and how they reflected images. It took him a while to realize that he was looking at his own reflection. That same day, I gave him a small mirror of his own. He spent the next several months holding it this way and that, checking out his face.

As his health improved, Thành was transferred from intensive care to a recovery room with ten beds. Each patient has his own caregiver so that made twenty of us cramped into a small communal room.

A withered old woman was in the bed next to Thành's. I slept on the floor between them. One night as she got up to get something in the cupboard I rose to offer help and she asked for a glass of water. As she raised it to her mouth, she went into convulsions, the glass slipping out of her hand. She fell over me. I helped her back to bed but by then she'd stopped moving. The commotion woke up the entire room.

I ran out to fetch the doctors. They arrived, ordered everybody out, and began to resuscitate her. By now her body was quite stiff. Thành did not want to leave the room. He asked, "Why waste all the effort? She's already dead." I finally convinced him to leave the room with the others. The doctors closed the door, reopening it forty-five minutes later only to wheel out a stretcher covered by a white sheet.

I noticed something special about Thành, he had a keen intuition which much more sensitive than others. In certain situations, he was more aware than most of us.

After three and a half months, Thành was completely recovered. The doctors discharged him; he could go home at any time. "But where?" we asked ourselves. I had no intention of taking him back to the psychiatric center. I decided to rent a room. Our friends at the hospital suggested that I should rent a place in suburban Saigon.

On the day we left several people gathered at the hospital gate to say farewell. We shook hands and hugged. A few people even brought small gifts for Thành.

Then someone tapped me on the shoulder. "Hey, before you leave, we'll baptize you," she said with a mischievous smile. Then, pointing to the hospital sign above us - BỆNH VIỆN TIM MẠCH - she added, "We'll call you 'Tim' from now on." "Tim" means "heart" in Vietnamese.

## *New Beginnings*

As we both started a new life, Thành and I moved into a small house in an under populated suburb northwest of the city. The roads leading to it were still plain dirt roads and the house was conveniently surrounded by banana gardens and lotus ponds.

That year I was twenty-two.

Everything was new to Thành and he had to learn everything from the beginning. Thành had to be part of a world which was totally strange to him. I promised myself to be a springboard for this unfortunate boy so that one day he could reach out to rediscover himself and to find a role to play in the community.

He did not know how to express himself. I would teach him how.

He could not read nor write. I would teach him so that he would have some basic knowledge.

He did not know how to participate in communal activities. I would introduce him to some friends, some brothers and sisters, and he would be part of an extended, caring family

Besides the hospital's light green uniform, Thành did not have any other clothes. So as soon as he was up and about, I took him shopping at Võ Thành Trang Market. It would be exciting for him, I thought, and this time he could choose his own clothing. At the market, however, Thành did not talk to anyone. Everything was as strange in his eyes as if he'd dropped down from another planet. He was indeed abandoned by his parents at birth, brought up by the religious nuns, and raised in a psychiatric center.

None of the clothes he was shown appealed to him, so I finally had to choose them on his behalf. Thành was uneasy in his new outfit. He'd never worn long pants before and he kept putting them on and taking them off alternately. When they were on, he'd roll them up above his knees. As we walked along he had a habit of yanking up his pants with both hands. I tried to explain that this wasn't going to work, and would he please try to leave his trousers alone. Clearly, he still had a long tough road ahead before he could feel at ease in a normal situation.

I shared with Thành the skill I knew best: painting. I taught him how to understand colors and how to use the brushes. His first paintings were brutal. He obsessively colored a series of black crosses dripping with blood or of Christ suffering; a dozen images but every one of the same theme with only two colors, red and black.

Thành laughed at me when he noticed my puzzlement over his bloody paintings. His laughter and the way he looked at me seemed sinister though. He was mimicking what he knew only too well, the madness of mental patients and the cruelty of the lost souls. And to emphasize the madness, he gleefully splashed more red paint to the canvas, repeating over and over again, "It's all blood, nothing but blood." I was desperately uncomfortable with this bizarre behavior, but I patiently let him continue, hoping he would be able to empty out all his pain and frustration and to start anew.

Thành was not used to personal hygiene and brushing his teeth was a torture. No wonder almost all his teeth were rotten. I tried to teach him how to clean his teeth, but he would not listen. He would just hold the brush in his mouth while tasting the tooth paste. He'd then shake his head to show his displeasure and immediately rinse out his mouth with lots of water. I reminded him about brushing before rinsing, but he would refuse point blank. The first few days he put on a tantrum when he had to clean his teeth.

Thành had to continue his treatment at home, something he bitterly resented. Whenever I gave him his pills, he pretended to swallow them, hiding them under his tongue and spitting them out the moment my back was turned.

His skin was still covered with sores, so twice a day I spread a petroleum-based balm over his very painful skin rash. And he did not like this one little bit either. However, I persisted with the treatment and slowly his elephant hide-like skin became softer.

One day when Thành was well I took him on the back of my bike for a trip to the city. On the way he observed everything carefully; the buildings, the roads, the shops and everything were strange to him. He asked: "Is this a church?" I answered "No, they are homes where families lived. These are the shops where they sell different goods, these are the hotels, and these are the restaurants."

## The Second Family Member

One evening, I took Thành to the Theater Minh Châu on Lê Văn Sỹ Street. While waiting in line for tickets, Thành spotted a boy in rags, begging. He made a funny face and said, "Don't give him anything!" "Why on earth not?" I said. "He's only run into some bad luck, just like you! That's why he needs to beg! I think we should give him a hand." And I invited the boy to watch the movie with us.

He was eleven years old, and I'd seen him around a few times before, sleeping on the sidewalks at noon under a blazing sun. He was completely on his own, trying to survive on the streets.

After the show, I asked Bình if he'd like to come and live with us. He instantly accepted. We agreed on the time and place for tomorrow's pick up since I could only carry one on my bike and Thành was already on the back seat!

Next day, Bình was right on time at the spot we'd agreed to meet. I took him home on my old bike. He was thin and famished but after he ate something, he happily took a tour of his new shelter. He liked to touch everything because he'd never seen so many household items before. He loved looking at the pictures in books. To him, it was just like a magic discovery.

Now it was Bình's turn to go to the market to get his personal things, some clothes and sandals. Unlike Thành, Bình knew exactly what he wanted. He had a hard time choosing; he liked too many things.

After a few days of community life, Bình opened his heart and told me his life story. Some time ago, Bình and his friend decided that they were sick of their wretched existence in the countryside and agreed they would travel to Saigon. Without tickets, they smuggled themselves onto a train and hid themselves on the roof of the train wagon. At a station somewhere in Central Vietnam they stole a chicken, then scrambled back to the roof to continue their journey. They were about to enjoy the chicken when the train was engulfed in a complete darkness. Emerging out into the day light, Bình found himself covered with blood and his friend was dead, decapitated as the train sped through the tunnel. Alone once again, Bình continued his journey to Saigon and melted into the big city crowds. He lived on the streets, slept under awnings, begged and fed himself on scraps and leftovers.

So now I lived in the house with two boys without identification papers. They both had a painful past but they both survived and overcame their hardships.

Bình was more mature than Thành. Street life had toughened him, and he took every opportunity to survive. While he was in the streets, no one cared.

The two boys got to know each other. I taught them about sharing, about compassion and about family life.

One day, Bình ran off with the radio boom box I'd given Thành before Bình had moved in. Thành was very angry. I went looking for the young criminal. I searched every place where he used to hang out, but in vain.

One day, when I had given up any hope of seeing Bình again, he came back and pulled out the radio with an embarrassed look on his face. "I miss you, I miss home. I'm sorry I took your radio, brother Thành, here it is back to you." Thành was still mad; he took the radio back and gave Bình a lecture on honesty. I explained to Thành the reason why he should forgive Bình. He had come back, which meant that he regretted what he had done, and he thought of us as family. Thành listened, calmed down, even smiled. He welcomed Bình back, ready to forgive and offer him a second chance to live together.

After his escape and return, Bình painted a nice a picture for us of trees in full bloom, with colors, and a bird on a branch.

I still had confidence in my two brothers. I felt I could help them to a good end. We were going to be a true family. I was ready to open our door to other disadvantaged children.

Nhân was next to arrive. A religious sister brought him over and she told me that Nhân's family was too poor to care for him. He was badly deformed, even at 18, he could not talk or walk, and neither could he close his mouth. His face was so deformed that he wore a permanent frown. He drooled, and it was difficult to feed him.

But for all these challenges, we did not give up. I taught Nhân drawing every day. At the beginning I had to hold his hand to guide him but slowly he could hold the pen himself. Every day I practiced talking to Nhân as well, I would say a word and Nhân would repeat it after me. Nhân could not walk but his legs were still strong, so I held his back and taught him to walk. Eventually, with our help, he managed to stand upright, to talk, and to draw.

After Nhân, we welcomed Phong, Điền, Lâm, Thúy, Trâm, and Kiệt. They were all either disabled or in poor health. I learned as much as I could about their health issues and I learned how to care for them. I ended up loving them all.

After six months my family of two had now increased to 13 members.

I started thinking hard about family financial affairs as well as how to make my family legitimate in the eyes of the government. From this point onwards, I understood my long-term responsibility and accepted my destiny to follow the road awaiting in front of me.

*A family meal in the first rented house (1994)*

*"By then my family had increased to 15. I became more interested in serious paralysis cases. Every day, after taking care of the children at home, I went to the hospital to visit the patients there. Then I went to the Franciscan Center to change the dressings for the paraplegic patients, and every now and then I went to the university."*

# CHAPTER 3

# Life and
# Its Side Tracks

One day on the way home from the market with Thành, I heard someone calling my name. It was the lady from one of the Christian charitable groups. On the back of her bicycle sat a man without legs known as Mr. Quy Cut. They were on their way to visit the severe paraplegic patients at a center almost two miles away. The man pleaded for me to come with them, so I joined them. We rode on bumpy dirt roads like in the countryside, crossed a vast cemetery and finally arrived at our destination. It was a very dark old house without even the most basic necessities and the stale smell of urine and sickness lingered in the air.

I came upon a row of beds occupied by ten or so young men, all with atrophied legs and I said hello to each one. They were surprised and happy to have visitors. Mr. Quy Cut, with an air of seriousness, said to me, "They're worse off than I am, they really need your help."

## Under the Roof of the Franciscan Center

This house was set up by the Franciscan Friars to provide care and shelter to their disabled patients, but without much financial support they could not offer anything else. The residents only had two rules to follow: a daily common prayer and lights out at 9 p.m. The majority of the paraplegic patients there were the result of work place accidents. They used to be strong men earning their living with their own strength. Suddenly their accidents happened, and they became disabled and immobile in their beds. They were in pain and they had no one to care for them. Most of them were only about my age and yet their future had been taken away from them.

On the way home, I thought more about those unfortunate young men. They were like my orphaned children; they were abandoned by their own family because they had become a burden to them. Physically they were in pain, but their emotional pain was much worse. They really needed a family.

The next day I returned to the Franciscan Center to comfort the young paralyzed patients with some food and, most importantly, to find out how I could help them. They showed me their bedsores, some old wounds with the skin hardened and shiny.

A generous surgeon offered to operate for free on Minh, one of the paraplegic patients. Sadly, due to lack of follow-up care, Minh developed an infection and the wound had reopened. It was an enormous wound with oozing puss.

For the first time that had volunteered as a nurse, I cleaned a wound. It was sizeable, and I could see the bone protruding from his buttocks. It took a while to clean and I must have used more than a dozen cotton balls to clean everything properly and cover the trauma with gauze.

## Room 212 of the Orthopaedic Trauma Center

The next day, Minh still had a high fever, so I took him to the emergency room at the Orthopaedic Trauma Center. Minh was admitted to Spinal Ward Room 212 which was reserved for patients with serious infections.

It was December 25, 1994, and Vietnam just came out of a long war in which it suffered so much loss. The country was still trying to modernize, to develop a free market economy, and to welcome foreigners back. I knew there was a gap in the social, cultural and educational experience but I strongly believed that I had found a place here. I believed that no matter who I was or what nationality I held or where I lived, human love and compassion knows no borders.

Room 212 had four old and tattered single beds. The patients here were very poor. Abandoned by their families, they depended on the kindness of the hospital staff and the religious groups for their simple meals, some soap for washing and a little pocket money. It helped but was never enough to help them completely recover. They used to be strong, handsome men, but smashed spinal cords had reduced them to paraplegic or quadriplegic immobility. They were helpless and dependent on others.

The three other patients lay on their stomachs, almost naked except for a pair of shorts tied on one side; elastic waistbands were banned to prevent their rubbing against the sores.

One young man, thin as a skeleton, had a large bandage on his back and behind. The rest of his body was raw flesh, devoid of skin.

Another patient had a cage-like metal frame surrounding his shaved head. It consisted of four rods—one fixed behind each ear, two more at the forehead and the back of the head and joined together at the top. The frame was attached to a rope and pulley installed at the head of the bed and beyond the bed hung a weight. The device was arranged to lift up the patient's head, thereby reducing the pressure on his displaced vertebrae. It would stay in place for weeks until a decision could be made whether or not to operate.

The third patient of Room 212 seemed to be in better shape. Still, my heart sank when the time came to clean his bedsores. The stench was so bad that the nurse waved everyone out of the room. I asked to stay behind so I could watch the procedure. The gaping wounds on his buttock begun forming fissures in the flesh and the infection had reached the bones from which the nurse carefully extracted fragments with a pair of tweezers.

Step by step, I was coming face to face with the devastating world of spinal injury victims in postwar Vietnam. If proper care wasn't available in time, they would inevitably succumb to infection or some other complication.

By then my family had increased to 15 and I became more interested in serious paralysis cases. Every day, after taking care of the children at home, I went to the hospital to visit the patients. Then I went to the Franciscan Center to change the dressings for the paralyzed patients and every now and then I went to the university, where I had enrolled to learn Vietnamese immediately after I met Thành. If I wished to know the needs of the people I wanted I help, then I should know how to speak their language. I was given a student tuition discount and it did not cost a lot. Furthermore, it gave me a one-year visa, so I could stay in Vietnam legally.

## The Unlucky Broken Bodies and Souls

I continued to regularly visit Minh, the boy I moved from the Franciscan Center to the Orthopaedic Trauma Center.

Minh's family was very poor and beginning when he was very little he had herded the water buffalo, chopped wood, and cleared land for planting crops. He ended up working for a well digging company. It was an ideal job for a strong man like Minh who could lift well over 300 pounds easily. But one day Minh fell into a deep well and his spinal cord was smashed. After the accident Minh lost half his weigh and now he weighed a mere 66 pounds.

When he was in the hospital he became friends with Tai, the third patient in Room 212.

Like Minh, Tai was once a strong, handsome young man. He was the bread winner for his family until the accident which made him a burden to his parents; he fell down from the top of a coconut palm. Work place accidents occurred daily, but the peasants would do anything to earn a few dollars no matter how dangerous it was. That year Tai was 24 and his parents were too old and frail to help him, they had to ask their neighbor to give Tai a hand to go down the river for bathing. And the leeches always enjoyed a feast from his open wounds

Days passed, and weeks passed, then months passed, and Tai's health deteriorated gradually. Finally, his parents and his neighbor cooked him a delicious meal and he smoked his last cigarette, just like the scene of the prisoner on death row having a last treat before his execution.

Then one afternoon, in desperation, Tai left the thatched hut in the middle of the Mekong Delta. He managed to get himself down to the river bank and dragged himself to a small boat. He didn't know where he was heading but he was determined to disappear and die alone. He rowed for a very long time, eventually drifting to the famous Phùng Hiệp floating market. The nuns from a local pagoda took him in for a few weeks, administering their traditional herbal medicines, but he failed to improve. By now he had heard about a trauma center in Saigon and that gave him hope.

He went to the bus station. He had no money. People took pity on him and a bus driver brought him all the way to Saigon. Tai found further help and was admitted to the hospital free of charge.

When Minh and Tai were ready to leave the Trauma Center, I suggested that they move into our house. Their accidents forced them to take another life turn, but I hoped I could help them to avoid a dead end and to find the road to rediscover their life balance.

"I dreamt that one day these children and these disabled residents would all have normal lives and would have a skill in their hands to keep themselves self-supporting. They would all have a cozy roof for their families and all would find a positive role to play in society."

# CHAPTER 4

## The Establishment of Maison Chance, the Lucky House at Binh Hung Hoa District

During this time, I started learning the Vietnamese language so that I could be more effective in caring for my family. I rescheduled the programs for Maison Chance activities to be more accurate and more complete. I had to work on a budget that could cover for all the expenditures for the house. I was always aware of the necessity of having sufficient funds to finance the lifelong project that I was planning.

I needed extra help to care for the children, so I employed two students who cooked the children's meals and who also taught them in some subjects. With this help I had time to plan for fundraising and other financial affairs.

I survived the first year thanks to the help from my family and proceeds from the sale of my paintings. My mother was a professional singer who had set up a charitable organization in Bolivia to help our less fortunate people. She used her organization and her singing classes to spread the story of Maison Chance and its needs. My grandmother and my uncle were also very supportive, both financially and emotionally.

Still, the expenses grew day by day. I began writing about my work, so I could spread the word to potential donors. I wrote in longhand and when finished, I put all my messages in between two cardboard sheets and rode my bike to the Post Office to fax my story to everyone I could think of, even though I had never met some of them. When I got to the Post Office I left my bicycle with the keeper on the pavement then went inside to join the long queue.

A single fax page cost a whopping 75,000 Vietnamese đồng, or the equivalent of 4.75 US dollars, while a bowl of rice noodle soup cost only 2,000 to 3000 đồng, or 08 to13 US cents. While at the Post Office, I often made use of the public telephone to stay in touch with family and friends in Switzerland. Oddly enough, I was not nostalgic even though I now lived in strange place more than 6,000 miles from my homeland.

I was twenty-two, and I felt as if I was Vietnamese already.

About this time an incident occurred at the rented house at Tan Binh District where my orphans lived. My landlord lived almost two miles away and visited us once a week. While at the house he always piled up the garbage at the back of our house and burned it. Thành watched all this with interest.

One day, he decided to imitate the landlord and burned a pile of rubbish close to the house. It happened to be in a field of dry grass which quickly caught fire. Luckily, we were able to put it out without causing too much damage, but the landlord was less than pleased and told me to find another place.

## *Vincent's Visit: My Brother Who Could not Hear*

At the end of 1995, Vincent, my younger brother, paid me a visit. He was going through a bad time, so I invited him to stay for a while and help with the handicapped and the orphans.

Vincent was only 19 months younger than me. He had been deaf since he was a child and I loved him dearly. I learned sign language to communicate with him and this helped me to appreciate the richness of human communication.

Vincent's handicap was actually a plus in Vietnam. He was able to communicate effectively with everybody by using sign and gestures. Besides dressing the residents' wounds, he taught them drawing. But, more often than not, his classroom was empty because he'd taken everybody out to play pool.

Everyone, the disabled as well as the kids, loved Vincent the first time they met, and they quickly christened him Vinh.

One evening, Vincent was on his motorcycle, shirtless, with Minh the paraplegic on the back seat. While riding across the cemetery they knocked over a cyclist. Minh was thrown through the air and landed unscathed about ten feet away. He ended up on the middle of the road chuckling heartily. By now the onlookers had crowded around. Minh could only stand up with the help of Vincent, who was himself covered all over with scratches and bruises. The child on the bike was not injured and the bike was only slightly damaged, so all we had to do was fix the bike. Everything was fine by the end.

A few years later, Minh named his first son Vinh, after Vincent.

## The Xôi *Vendor and the New House at Binh Hung Hoa*

Besides the two employed students I found another woman helper. She was divorced from her husband and lived with her four small kids.

I first met her on Lê Văn Sỹ Street selling *xôi*—cooked glutinous rice—from a large container mounted on her bicycle. The sticky rice was arranged in an attractive rainbow of colors—orange, purple, yellow, brown and white—each denoting a different flavor. Individual portions were served on a piece of banana leaf and topped with crushed peanuts, sesame seeds and shaved coconut.

She and her children were very poor, so she was curious about the orphaned children under my care. She and her kids lived in a ghetto that had grown up among some old neglected graves on the outskirt of a nearby town where the Catholic refugees had settled and built a large Catholic church. The Catholics had moved here from the north in the years 1954 and 1955, after the Geneva Agreement divided the country into North and South Vietnam.

Soon after we became acquainted, the *xôi* vendor began visiting us regularly bringing her bowls, spoons and chopsticks and cooking for the entire household. I finally officially hired her and put her in charge of meals and grocery shopping.

The landlord did not forget about the fire and he insisted that we move out as soon as possible.

One evening as I rode to the Franciscan Center, an idea occurred to me. Why didn't I look for a home closer to the paralyzed patients? Every day I rode about six miles to visit the patients and if I were nearer to them, it would be much more convenient. Luckily a Franciscan Center patient told me that there was a duplex for sale in nearby Binh Hung Hoa village. Here was our chance.

I offered to buy half of the property first and agreed that would buy the second half when I had saved up enough money. The seller agreed to my offer. The unit measured approximately 13 feet wide by slightly over 42 feet long and could comfortably accommodate ten or so people. I promptly bought it for the equivalent of 2,000 US dollars. At the time, banks weren't popular in Vietnam, so people kept their valuables at home, usually in the form of jewellery. My seller wanted payment in gold and I obliged, scouring the market for gold rings. And since Vietnamese law did not allow foreigners like me to own real estate, the house was registered in the name of the former *xôi* vendor, in whom I had absolute trust.

We moved in during February 1995, just before *Tết*, the Vietnamese New Year.

For all of us, it was urgent that we have a roof over our heads, food in our bellies, and access to medical care. But what we needed most was vocational training for a job.

I wished to offer the less fortunate a better life in the future and to provide them with a skill, so they could be independent in spite of their initial challenges.

I dreamt that one day these children and these disabled residents would all have normal lives and would have a skill in their hands to keep themselves self-supporting. They would have a cozy roof for their families and all would find a positive role to play in society.

Since they were all illiterate no regular school would accept them, we began home-schooling them ourselves to wipe out illiteracy among our people. The *xôi* vendor, who could read, write and count reasonably well, would teach them to read, write and to learn basic math while I took care of teaching French and drawing.

## The Thatched Hut and New Family Members

For over a year I had been caring for the spinal injury patients at the Trauma Center, but when they were discharged they had nowhere to go. Their families were so poor that they were unable to care for them and these former patients were practically abandoned without the means to survive.

Some of the long-term sufferers did not want to carry on living.

Right in front of our house, there was a vacant block of land bordered by the wastewater channel. Behind this block of land was a thatched hut for rent. I signed a lease to rent the hut for the paralyzed residents and soon after we welcomed Hát, Lánh, Tai, Minh, Thành, Sy, Ông Ru, Trung, Mon, Hien, Thang, Quang, Thịnh Trung. Most were victims of work accidents and then abandoned. Some were in a post-surgical state while others had unhealed wounds. But all were permanently paralyzed and had to lie on their backs for no one knew for how long.

First, I had to renovate the bathroom to make it accessible to the handicapped.

We built a chair with a cut out in the seat to use in the shower and we enlarged the entrance door for wheelchair access. And we also acquired a bed on wheels to assist those unable to sit up.

Some people could be independent but the majority need assistance. I trained my adopted children how to care for the paralyzed patients; for example, how to carry them around and how to help push their wheelchairs. The patients also needed physiotherapy treatment as well to keep their muscles working and they needed to move to avoid the hardening of the joints.

With this arrangement, during the day the young and healthy could have a job caring for the paralyzed patients and in return the adult handicapped could share their life experiences and guide their young helpers with their wisdom.

In their daily lives the two generations shared one roof, helping one another and together they created a harmonious family atmosphere. The orphans and the handicapped both shared a painful, unhappy past but this helped to bring them closer together and they felt comfortable living under one roof.

Between the common room and the bathroom was a stinky old pigsty, so I asked the owner for permission to modify it into our music room. Later on, I built a small hut for a painting studio.

*The handicapped on their crutches photographed in front of the house on the hand-built bridge.*

During the wet season, the yard became muddy and wheelchairs could not use it. But I had the whole inside floor and the area around the house cemented so it could be used all the year round.

Meals were cooked in the main house and it was a tricky business carrying large pots and pans over the wastewater channel every day. Eventually, we bridged the channel gap using two panels removed from a donated billiard table. Now we had a proper bridge to join the two houses.

The number of patients at Maison Chance increased steadily. I was enthusiastically researching new medications, boning up on nursing and caring for the handicapped, and consulting both local and overseas specialists wherever possible, especially regarding the treatment of spinal cord injuries. My letters to potential donors abroad bore fruit and my efforts brought several shipments of medical supplies.

I hired a carpenter to build a medicine cabinet to be placed in the rented house where it would be most needed. It came with a lock and key and I alone distributed the medicines since the directions for their use were virtually all in French and I was the only one who could read French then.

## A Lesson in Trust

Trust was the operative word at Maison Chance; we operated our house as a family.

When the *xôi*-vendor (now the legal house owner) returned from the market, she gave me any change she had left over, and it never occurred to me to ask about expenses or receipts. It was the honour system all the way.

But then an unthinkable incident happened. While I was in Europe, the *xôi*-vendor was seduced by the carpenter I had hired to do some work in the house. The couple pretended to have been burgled and also made a claim for wages which I had already settled before my departure.

At that time, I was still a bit naïve and I never asked for receipts for any purchases, therefore I had no evidence or proof of payment of any kind.

At the same time, the *xôi*-vendor kidnapped a child and hid her in another house, then claimed that the child had run away after she was caught stealing goods at the shop. The *xôi*-vendor also reminded me that the house was in her name and she demanded that I take the all the children and leave the premises.

We had no choice but to comply and we moved into the rented house while I filed a complaint. I listed all the criminal acts committed by the *xôi*-vendor, a person that I fully trusted but who turned out to be a liar, a kidnapper and a thief. But no sooner had we contacted the police than the couple vanished. I never heard from them again. In the end, the court decided in our favor.

The experience taught me that while empathy was a good thing, blind trust was altogether different.

We moved back into our house. At the back of the house was a store room which I renovated and made into a dormitory for the healthy young boys. I had windows and insect screens installed plus four built-in bunk beds. Two boys shared one bed.

Between the orphans and the handicapped, I had more work than I could handle so I found a helper, a former patient at the hospital. He'd suffered from Pott's disease (spinal tuberculosis) but thanks to timely surgery he was able to walk again. After convalescence, he decided to stay at the hospital to help take care of the handicapped patients and that was how we met.

His experience and knowledge of spinal-cord injuries was immensely valuable. Together we managed to have equipment built to get our disabled residents back on their feet, including standing beds for the quadriplegics and parallel bars with leg braces for the paraplegics. He was an expert in caring for spinal cord patients and he knew how to teach them to stand up and walk.

## Teacher Tùng and the Birth of the First New School

Another new collaborator of mine was Thay Tùng, a schoolteacher.

Mr. Tùng and his two emaciated, handicapped sons had washed up at Maison Chance not so long before. The older son was my age. He was a good poet and he gave me a poem about a butterfly spreading happiness as it fluttered about.

The condition of the two brothers grew considerably worse and there was no hospital to care for them. They were deeply attached to each other and died within a few months of each other. At the funeral of his elder son, Mr. Tùng screamed like a man possessed. But after a period of grieving, he decided to devote himself to the care of the handicapped at Maison Chance.

Since Mr. Tùng was a trained schoolteacher I invited him to stay on and he joined us as the school principal.

We had only a single classroom and it was getting too small for the number of students, so I applied for and was granted the use of an adjacent vacant lot that belonged to the city. It would have to be returned whenever they needed it. So, with much help from our kids who tirelessly transported bricks, sand and cement, we built a second classroom.

I hired a second teacher, a young woman from the North. Our school gradually took shape with two teachers, two classrooms, and forty students, aged from ten to forty. The majority of the students had never sat on a school bench before and had no idea about classroom protocol or discipline. Notions like the duration of classes—at least forty-five minutes—refraining from interrupting the teacher and seeking the teacher's permission before leaving the room were all mysteries to the students.

## No Walls Could Separate Us

We'd been renting the thatched hut for a year now and had made extensive renovations, furnishing it to accommodate our disabled residents as comfortably as could be. We hoped to stay there for the long time.

One day, however, the landlady invited me to her house and informed me that she had to pay taxes and that a new law obliged her to modify our contract. She asked me to pay the rent right through to the end of the year, or seven months' worth all at one time. I was unconvinced and said I expected her to honor the original

*The first family photo, taken in front of the rented house, July 1995.*

agreement. Clearly, her nose was out of joint and she began to make daily life difficult, threatening to cut the water supply.

Then she had a wall erected on the empty lot which separated her property from mine. Her fence isolated the thatched hut, so we were forced to go around this wall to move back and forth between the hut and the main house, a detour which made the trip four times longer. It was still the rainy season and the uneven road became slippery with mud so transferring the pots and pans at mealtimes became extremely treacherous. The conditions were even worse for the people in wheelchairs. They unfailingly landed flat in the mud as their wheelchairs capsized. Our landlady never lifted a finger; she just stared at the children as they struggled to lift up the fallen and as they later helped the handicapped to wash their muddy clothes.

Everyone stayed calm looking for a solution, except for Thành. My young brother was more immature than other kids his age and Thành couldn't contain his anger. He threw cow dung in the landlady's drinking-water tank and threatened to burn down the house. Visibly alarmed, she asked me to replace the thatched roof with tin, and I complied.

One morning, while looking at the thatched hut, I noticed a new "For Sale" sign with a telephone number posted on the wall of the small, vacant house next to the thatched hut. I called and spoke to the owner. He manufactured fine mother-of-pearl furniture and wood carvings of all sorts—including Buddha figures and the four sacred animals: dragons, unicorns, turtles and phoenixes. He also owned a retail store on Cộng Hòa Avenue to display his products.

He had planned to use the house that he now had for sale to manufacture lacquerware, but the structure was too small for this purpose. I told him about Maison Chance and what we planned to do with his house. He was moved by our story and offered us the use of his block of land and the house until I'd raised enough money to buy the entire 4,500-square-foot property.

This block of land was right in front of the rented house for the orphans.

Now Maison Chance occupied three abutting lots. Eventually, though, I knew we'd have to move out of the rented house. The number of residents was growing each day and it would only make sense to construct a larger facility.

The problem was that we'd need a building permit and, in 1995 as a foreigner, I didn't qualify for one. Moreover, I was still in the process of legalising my family's status. I needed to look for an alternative strategy, so I resorted to the same perfectly legal tactics used by all Vietnamese. I would ask for permission to erect an enclosure wall around our two properties and then later build a wooden structure, for which no permit was required, inside the compound.

I decided to do just that, subject to the village mayor's approval, of course. I had always addressed this lady as "maire" (French for mayor and pronounced exactly like the French word for mother,

*The small house (Later Maison Chance or the Lucky House) on the 1,380 square feet of land in between the old house (left) and the rented house (right) in 1995.*

*mère*). "You know," she said, "of the tens of thousands of people in this village, you're the only one who ever calls me 'mother'. I like that. So, go ahead and build your wall. I'm behind you all the way!"

Heartened by her support, we set to work. Our new parcel of land had been neglected for years. It was marshy and overrun with tall grass. So, I mobilized all hands on-deck, including Thành. They sprayed the soil, jumped up and down to flatten the ground, carried bricks, and generally pitched in. Once the wall was up, however, I decided to simply install a tin roof that extended from the main house as far as the wall and to tile the floor. Welcome to our new shelter! We moved the first beds for our disabled residents.

There were now more than fifty people living together like a family, though we weren't actually related to one another. Our situation was indeed precarious, yet this situation encouraged mutual assistance and gave us the courage to confront the challenges we faced.

As 1996 drew to a close, we were celebrating the Tết New Year on the piece of land where Maison Chance would put down its roots.

*"The construction was almost finished.
All it needed now was a coat of paint. Ever since
I was a little girl, I had always enjoyed playing
with colors and so I chose a special color for
my family: the color blue, the color of hope.
We painted the entire outer fence of
Maison Chance in the color of sky blue."*

# CHAPTER 5

# The Birth of NGO Maison Chance

One morning a governmental inspection team showed up at our construction site. They were representatives from various departments such as Building and Construction, Education, Health, Police, and Treasury. After I'd answered every question they asked, they wrote down what I'd said and read it back to me. It all sounded right, so I signed the document and they gave me a copy. Looking at it later, I realized that it didn't quite reflect my answers. They correctly noted that I didn't have a permit to administer medical treatment to handicapped patients but failed to note that we were only providing them shelter and that all necessary medical treatments were carried out by doctors and specialists at the hospital.

The very next day an article appeared in the local newspaper reporting the discovery of a medical center being operated without a licence by a Swiss citizen named Aline Rebeaud.

Soon afterward, I got a letter from the District People's Committee citing my offence. I was given two weeks to dismantle Maison

Chance and relocate all occupants; the children were to be sent back to the orphanages and the disabled residents back to the hospitals.

My response was "No, this should not happen."

I immediately wrote a three-page reply explaining that Maison Chance was taking care of individuals who had been abandoned by all services. The children were too old to be admitted to orphanages while the handicapped had already been discharged by the hospital. I asked for a meeting with the relevant authorities to negotiate a solution and to untangle our legal status.

I was given two weeks to defend my case.

## A Nerve-wracking Two Weeks

The next two weeks were hectic, and I got very little sleep. The police summoned me constantly to answer their questions. I had to answer both orally and in writing and I was confronted by the same questions over and over again. I made sure that my answers were complete and truthful.

By now I had stopped attending formal Vietnamese classes and I hoped my street lessons would help me to master the language. But, I was also back to the University as often as I could to catch up with my university professor for advice and guidance on the best Vietnamese words and phrases to use in approaching governmental authorities.

As soon as my initial drafts to the People's Committee of Binh Chanh District seemed reasonable, I took them to a public scribe for editing and inputting into his computer. He was a charming young man, so deeply focused on his work that sometimes I had to wait at his house until two or three in the morning as he finished typing my scribbled longhand letter. And riding home at that hour through the dark, thief-infested cemetery was not much fun.

The situation became serious and urgent. I had to ask for help from the Swiss Embassy in Vietnam.

The next thing I knew, high-ranking officials from the Ministry of the Interior in Hanoi descended on Saigon to investigate our case. They interviewed the spinal- ward doctors who had treated our disabled residents. The atmosphere was tense, and my doctor friends were worried for Maison Chance. But when the officials finally came to pay us a visit, they saw with their own eyes how sympathetically we looked after our charges. I dared to hope that at the very least they understood that Maison Chance was truly and honestly a non-profit organisation.

Still, nothing was settled and the deadline for dismantling Maison Chance was only a few days away. The residents were getting nervous and restless, ready to march to the District People's Committee and fight for our existence. I talked them out of it and decided to approach the Swiss Consulate for help.

It turned out to be a good move. I was promptly granted an interview with Mr. Phạm Phương Thảo, then Vice-President of the City People's Committee, who was in charge of social services. Finally, my case was going to be heard by someone in authority!

The meeting took place at City Hall, an ornate building dating back to French colonial times, and the Swiss Consul came with me. Once the initial formalities were over, we were escorted to the appointed room where, to our surprise, the Vice-President was accompanied by about dozen solemn-looking functionaries, some of whom I'd met before. Needless to say, my hopes of confiding in the Vice-President informally one-on-one vanished!

She was sitting on an imposing carved-wooden chair. We were placed directly to her left and the functionaries sat opposite us. The Vice-President spoke first and then the Swiss Consul introduced me. The future of Maison Chance depended on this meeting and I knew

I had to weigh my words carefully and make a good impression. The officials had every reason to be concerned. After all, I was a mere foreigner in their country, with no official affiliation whatsoever. All I possessed was my good faith. And so, I laid everything out with as much enthusiasm as I could muster, perhaps even overdoing things a little because the Consul kept nudging me with his elbow.

The meeting ended without a decision, but at least I had been heard. We were now less than two days away from the deadline issued by the District authority to dismantle Maison Chance. We had no idea what would happen. We imagined jeeps filled with police officers arriving to tear down the building. Nevertheless, we clung to our hopes. The orphans and the handicapped were ready to defend their home and their family by every available means.

During these nerve-wracking two weeks of fighting against the clock, I spent every ounce of energy I had writing letters and attending each and every meeting to which I was summoned. I was as straightforward as possible in telling my story—who I was, what I was trying to do, and why I was doing it. It was exhausting, but I kept faith in the rightness of our cause.

When the fateful day came, we were all gathered in front of the house, ready to protest. There wasn't a single jeep in sight. The atmosphere was tense, though. Hours passed, we stayed alert, but nothing happened. A few days later, a letter arrived from the District People's Committee saying that they'd suspended the injunction to dissolve Maison Chance.

## The Establishment of Maison Chance as an NGO

So, for the time being at least, the authorities had allowed me to keep running Maison Chance, which I'd built up from scratch in the first place. But until it gained official and legal recognition, I knew

I had a fierce battle on my hands; one that might persist for years. However, this was a good lesson for me concerning patience.

At the time, Vietnam had just opened itself up to the outside world and my case was unprecedented. I was an unaffiliated, twenty-five-year-old foreign national running a home for the destitute in a fledgling country. There were, in fact, no legal provisions and the authorities were hesitant. Maison Chance with a European at its helm presented a dilemma.

And that explains why I was constantly interviewed and queried by the police at every level—village, district, and city. I spent hours discussing the purpose of Maison Chance, my reasons for staying, and how I envisioned the future.

At the same time, I initiated meetings with government agencies dealing with social issues and foreign relations, exploring ways for Maison Chance to go forward. One possible solution was to organize it as a foreign NGO with a permit to operate in Vietnam. I'd have a head start since I already had a network of donors in both Switzerland and France.

I approached the Swiss Embassy about registering Maison Chance in my native country. But that wasn't a suitable option because Swiss law did not require non-profit associations to register in the first place. As luck would have it, in early 1997 France's *Journal Officiel* had listed Maison Chance as an *Association Loi 1901*—an expression used by the French to designate a not-for-profit entity—sponsored by the Rhône-Alpes Prefecture. With this information, I was able to present myself to the Vietnamese authorities as the representative of an NGO officially recognized by a foreign state.

(Non-Governmental Organizations, commonly referred to as NGOs, are generally non-profit and sometimes international organizations that are independent of governments and international governmental organizations. NGOs are typically active in promoting healthcare, humanitarian, educational, public policy, social, human rights, and environmental activities.)

At the end of 1996, I returned to Europe to establish Maison Chance (or Nha May Man in Vietnamese) there. I returned to Vietnam at the beginning of 1997 with a completed document stating that Maison Chance was a NGO registered abroad.

However, that was not enough. There was one more hurdle. In order to operate in Vietnam, we required a local partner. The Red Cross in our district had been mandated to serve as that partner and we were obliged to enter into a three-year cooperation agreement with them. I had no other choice, but neither was I ready to sign anything just yet. Far more important was my desire to maintain my freedom of action. Negotiations lasted over a year before I was able to conclude the Red Cross contract.

## *Lady Michelham: The Helping Hands*

I was in the process of finishing off the construction of the building for the handicapped residents when I ran out of money.

Luckily one of the thousands of letters I sent overseas came into the hands of Lady Michelham of Hellingly, a lady full of wisdom. Her husband had been a wealthy English aristocrat who was 40 years her senior, and Lady Michelham and her husband used some of their funds to sponsor their own charity before he died. Upon his passing, she had inherited the whole of her husband's fortune.

Born in Northern France, Lady Michelham had suffered from tuberculosis of the bones as a child but eventually recovered after being bed-ridden, and later in a wheelchair, for many years. She completed her studies and became a social worker with a primary interest in paraplegia. She understood exactly what I was doing in Vietnam. She wrote to say that the Michelham of Hellingly

*The Maison Chance family in the courtyard of the wooden house in July 1997.*

Foundation would take care of the building expenditures and costs—a whopping 80 percent as it turned out. The amount of her contribution was 40,000 US dollars!

The construction was almost finished. All it needed now was a coat of paint. Ever since I was a little girl, I had always enjoyed playing with colors and so I chose a special color for my family: the color blue, the color of hope. We painted the entire outer fence of Maison Chance in the color of sky blue.

At that time Maison Chance had around 60 residents, not to mention scores of other people who turned up regularly for temporary assistance.

## The Urbanization of Country Life

The village of Binh Hung Hoa was rapidly developing and it attracted thousands of job seekers from North and Central Vietnam who came in search of affordable housing. But while new houses sprang up like mushrooms, the roads remained unpaved, electricity was haphazard, and the sewage system was nonexistent. And hardly any infrastructure was being planned.

Once again, the children were set to work laying a drainpipe between the two buildings and the small canal that ran through the village. So much garbage was being dumped into the canal that it soon became known as 'the black canal'.

Social life in the neighborhood was lively. People left their doors open and private lives quickly became a public affair. One day, a horse fell into the canal and the whole village came to the rescue. The operation took all afternoon as time here was elastic and people made themselves available when they felt like it, a notion utterly foreign to those of us conditioned by the rhythm of a Swiss clock.

From time to time, I'd noticed a colorful flag flying at the entrance to an alleyway. I soon learned that it was there to signal a death, serving in fact as a public announcement. Thus informed, friends and neighbors would rally round the deceased's family to pay their respects.

I also saw parents beating their kids in front of their homes. It was one of their customs and so they must have felt that such disciplinary measures were useful and necessary. But I myself believed that violence would only make things worse. My conviction was reinforced by the suffering of the mistreated children I'd taken under my wing and whom I hoped to heal and help reach their potential someday.

*Hát and Tai learning to walk on crutches in front of the Blue House.*

We'd paved the front courtyard in order to make things easier for our disabled residents; however, it hadn't quite worked out as we had planned. Our next-door neighbor insisted on herding her cows on the paved section and they dropped their dung along the way as they progressed. I did my best to persuade her to use the parallel dirt path, but she remained unconvinced and continued to promenade with her animals in front of our house. For some reason my attempts at describing how cow dung stuck to the wheels and then to the hands of the wheelchair riders were beyond her. There was nothing to do except be patient until she finally caught on.

## Hát and His First Computer

Keeping pace with the village of Binh Hung Hoa, Maison Chance was also expanding. By now there were ten employees working at Maison Chance. They were teachers, doctors, health care specialists and other miscellaneous workers. I concentrated on my managerial tasks and tried to modernize the Maison Chance administrative office. I bought a computer, so I could keep my books and write my letters and I did not have to take my work to be typed outside.

I learned computation with Hát, the 30-year-old patient whom I met in the spinal ward at the Orthopaedic Trauma Center. He was 19 when a truckload of stones fell on him at work, crushing his limbs. He was brought to the trauma center and ended up in Room 212 of the spinal ward and that was where we met in 1994. His family was unable to pay for his care and so he came to Maison Chance after his discharge from the hospital.

Hát was dynamic and we worked well together, developing and organizing files on the computer. I worked with Hát on accounts, management and the organisation of other internal affairs. The old printer came in handy, even though it made a lot of noise and frequently jammed. Needless to say, it was replaced as soon as we could afford a new one.

I felt happy seeing the residents at Maison Chance assume their responsibility in assisting me to build a happy family.

## The Contribution of Bart Dorsa

Bart Dorsa was a 33-year-old American with a head shorn like a monk. His mother was battling cancer, and he had his hair shaved in sympathy with his mother. He was the president of an American charity helping the poor children in Vietnam.

Bart had been to see us, and eventually decided to support our home. He pledged 3,000 US dollars a month for two years, a sum that represented 75 percent of our operating expenses.

Bart had also introduced me to Tim Bond who was then the representative of Saigon Terre des Hommes. Tim was an Englishman of my mother's age, born in 1948. He was managing several projects in developing countries, and I was grateful to have his support in developing our accounting system and our operating program as well as in helping us secure our official status in Vietnam. With his help, Maison Chance finally received its official status as an NGO in 1998. We were at last recognized by the Vietnamese authorities, with a permit to operate decreed by Hanoi.

## Arguments with The Red Cross

Our partnership with the local Red Cross was rather like a shotgun marriage. Neither party had been enthusiastic; not me and not the Red Cross president.

And it was hardly a marriage of equals. Whatever I wished to do had to be approved by Red Cross management, our local partners. But the director, originally from Ben Tre, was timid and fearful of making any decisions on her own. She sought opinions from the People's Committee and from the local police department and in turn, they summoned me in for questioning. Every project had to be in writing and handed on to the Director. She would pass it to the local People's Committee for opinions!!!!

Whether it was approved or not, it always took a few days before I received a piece of paper with the red stamp and signed by her. Without this red stamp I could do nothing!

From Maison Chance to the Red Cross Office was a distance of over six miles on a bad dirt road that took me two hours for each visit. Whenever I made this trip in the hot sticky weather of Vietnam, I turned up sweaty and covered with dirt. It took me some time to make myself presentable before I saw Madame the Director.

By contrast, the Red Cross Director hardly ever visited Maison Chance and then only on special occasions. She was about 45 years old and, like me, she did not have the option of choosing me to be her working partner.

The main duties of the Red Cross were organising a blood donation day and providing emergency services when there were natural disasters such as floods and storms. The Director lacked any experience in caring for orphans, disabled patients or homeless people. She only had to oversee our approved projects, which I had carefully documented word-by-word.

After a few months, I received a letter from the District authority appointing yet another lady who was going to help manage me Maison Chance as my partner. This position was not mentioned in the original contract where it was emphasized that I would be Maison Chance's sole manager.

But I did not have time to protest. The next morning, the said lady turned up claiming she was going to work at Maison Chance from now on.

I had no authority to throw her out. I hoped she could be of some use to us, but it appears all she wished to do was to spy on me, taking down all the contact numbers of people to whom I talked or sent faxes. The atmosphere in the Maison Chance front office was heavy.

While working at Maison Chance, the lady got involved emotionally with a paraplegic patent who I cared for daily and who was a few years younger than me. He had been stabbed while he was in an unsafe area.

One day the lady came into my office, stood in front of me and started shouting at me. I took a few steps back, using my hand to keep us apart. She stepped front of me and shouted at the top of her voice, "Tim beat me up. I am in pain!"

My office door was open and the paraplegic who was involved with the lady was waiting in his wheelchair just outside my door. As soon as he heard her shouting he wheeled himself out to the front of the building and cried out, "Tim beat up people."

The whole episode was surreal. Over the next few days, I tried talking to them, but I was rebuffed. They preferred to spend their time writing in their corner. That bothered me a little, but I was absorbed in my daily routine. Later I learned that they'd been busy writing up a complaint, which they subsequently sent to police departments at every level—village, district and city.

Once again, I was called in and subjected to a lengthy interrogation. I answered their questions as honestly as possible. I had lots of experience in this area and I didn't need to invent anything because the allegations were baseless. I was accused of attacking a Red Cross representative as well as of starving and depriving a handicapped resident of much needed medical treatment.

Clearly the goal was to make me look incompetent. I was hurt by my protégé's attitude; it was as if the woman had cast a spell on him. But Maison Chance's existence was now at risk and I knew I had to respond. Like a mother protecting her young, I fought back as forcefully as I knew how by spreading my own version of the events to the powers that be, all the way up to the Foreign Affairs Ministry.

The next few weeks were tense, but eventually my intervention produced an effect. The police ordered the Red Cross representative and her accomplice to vacate the premises and he was transferred to a place with which we were all familiar: the Franciscan Center for the Disabled.

It was a painful experience and it broke my heart. But my daily responsibilities didn't give me time to feel sorry for myself. And it was genuinely gratifying to see the Maison Chance residents going about their active weekly schedules cheerfully and energetically. Life slowly resumed its normal course.

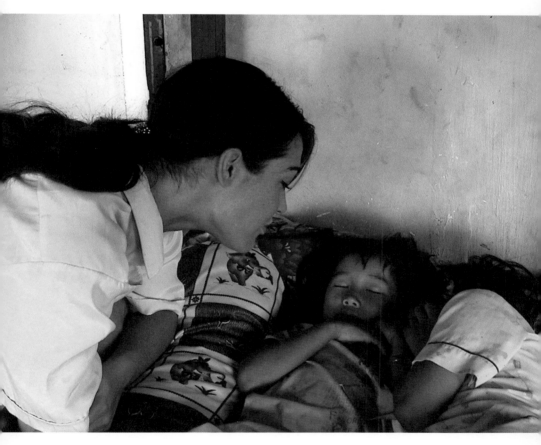

*Tim putting her child to bed.*

*"With time and the love of every member of our family, they were all aware of a new life vision and from this point onward, the unlucky handicapped people would step up from the bottom rung of the ladder."*

# CHAPTER 6

# The Elimination of Illiteracy and the First Vocational Training Class

Our school welcomed all of the Maison Chance residents as well as all local disadvantaged kids free of charge. These kids were over the age to be admitted into normal public school. The poor kids came mostly from a shanty town a half mile away which was over-populated with working people, most of whom were sight-impaired individuals.

## Children of the Blind

This sight-impaired community was supported previously by an Austrian charity named Caritas; however, the organization had stopped operations in Vietnam in the 1970's.

When Caritas was still in operation, this organization had built a center to teach trades, such as manufacturing brushes, at Binh Hung Hoa. Most of the sight impaired people of Caritas were now grownups and some had married other sight impaired partners.

When Caritas stopped operating, some residents kept on manufacturing brushes, but others could not find any jobs and ended up being beggars.

Mostof the children of sight impaired couples had perfect eyesight and they became the eyes and hands of their parents, guiding them to sell their products. But when their families ran into difficulty, the children had to beg too; they had no education and no support allowing them to be equal in society.

Every morning there was a long queue of blind people with their children guiding them. They were selling their brushes, performing songs and dances in the streets for their living or just simply begging, depending on the generosity of the public.

## French Lessons

The children and the disabled in our classes all needed to improve their education and social skills, so we paid close attention to mathematics and Vietnamese language classes. But besides these, we also offered studies in painting, music, and foreign languages. French was the most popular since most of our beneficiaries spoke French. From the beginning and until 1999, I personally ran the French class after which I appointed a French-educated lady of 50 to teach French on my behalf.

I was hoping the students who were good at foreign languages would specialize in learning French so later on they could earn a living by being translators, a very suitable profession for the disabled. But over the decades since war's end, the Vietnamese were eager to learn English, and nobody was interested in French except the older generation who spoke it in an outdated style. I needed to train someone who could speak and translate the current French language, but I had not found anyone yet.

At the end of each day, I gathered everyone in the physical-therapy room to teach and practice French, my mother tongue. The students eventually got the basics down pat and were able to communicate with our French-speaking visitors.

During this time, I was in a state of financial difficulty, but I managed to provide all the required needs of every member of Maison Chance. They had a roof over their head, food to fill their bellies and necessary medical care. But that was not enough.

I wished to provide the opportunity for each of them to develop to their own ability since this would help them become useful and respected by society. To achieve this aim, they had to be taught a basic knowledge and then introduced to trade training classes. But since most of them were physically challenged and some of them were too old to start, I had to find a solution for this problem.

## *Art Classes and the First Results*

One of the things I knew best was drawing and painting. I had been sharing this skill with my students and at the start painting was a therapeutic activity; it helped people to express their inner feelings. But my goal was that by the end of their training, they could create their own works and make a living from the sale of their products.

We began with handmade greeting cards and, of course, some residents were talented, and some were not. We gave each a job depending on their natural skills. Their products were at first badly produced so we had to regroup and most of their initial works ended up in the recycled paper bin.

*The school in the Blue House in 2005*

But even though this project did not succeed I was pleased. This exercise helped the time pass faster and it helped them to forget their physical pain. They also felt that they were not useless after all and that they could produce something worthwhile. Before long, we made Christmas cards for our sponsors and for sale in Europe. Through our associations in France and Switzerland, everyone involved in this activity received a symbolic salary. It was a boost to their self-esteem and their daily life definitely acquired a more joyful tone.

## The Sewing Room

After the painting class, I searched for other possible vocations which could be suitable for different students.

We opened the sewing room next. It turned out to be an ideal occupation for our paraplegic residents because the activity itself was stationary and required no physical strength. All we had to do was redesign the foot pedals so that they could be operated by an elbow instead of a person's feet.

However, neither painting nor sewing was suitable for the quadriplegics because their fingers were paralyzed so they could not hold the brushes or the needles.

## A Typing Career

One day a French Belgium gentleman who specialized in computer science turned up. He also had his own small charity. He had spinal column injury as well, but he was very lucky because he was the rare case who was cured due to medical innovation. However, he still had to walk with a stick. He was impressed with our achievements and promised to send computers from France to us, and so our computer room began. From that time going forward, our people with severe paralysis could contribute something as well. For example, we tinkered with the keyboard so that our severely paralyzed residents could type with a wooden stick attached to the palm of their hands.

Computers had just begun to make an appearance in Vietnam. Few people knew how to use them, never mind having one at home. Those lucky enough to own one earned a living by typing and printing different kinds of documents for a fee. I knew that once they were properly trained, our students would get all the work they could handle because the demand for such services was high. Ordinary people were obliged to write or apply for a variety of documents—residence and building permits, title deeds, and so on—but not everyone could produce the required documents on their own.

Although our workshops were still not fully productive, student morale improved as these new activities gave added meaning to their lives.

## *Overcoming All Desperation*

Our family had come a long way since arriving at Maison Chance. Each resident had been seriously ill, abandoned by their families and completely dependent on the kindness of others for survival. Many had even tried to take their own lives. Some remained severely depressed about their perceived worthlessness after they'd moved in with us. One had slashed his wrist, another slit the length of his leg with a knife, and a third—a quadriplegic—bit off one of his fingers on a Christmas Day. Fortunately, in each case we were able to intervene in the nick of time.

Then, just when things began to improve, a rickshaw driver appeared at our door with one of our paraplegic residents. His passenger was unconscious and delirious after swallowing hundreds of pills that somebody had given him. Phước, one of the orphans, was with me at the time. He lighted an incense stick and prayed aloud: "Heaven, thank you for letting our brother come back to us; he was suffering and is not well. Thank you for helping him get better, thank you for protecting our home. Help us overcome the tribulations in our lives."

It was as if they'd lost everything. I tried to convince them to stay hopeful; they still had their spirit and their intelligence. Together we'd walk them through to a brighter future. They would have to accept their physical disabilities, and in doing so, they would develop their minds. This way of thinking was new for them. They'd come from places where it was impossible to imagine a decent life when disabled. Yet, with time, and the affection of everyone in our family, their outlook on life was starting to renew itself.

## The Training Center Project

By 1999, we had three vocational workshops, all staffed with professional trainers, including a Vietnamese teacher who took over my French classes. She was 50 years old and had been to a French school.

At the same time, we were drastically running out of space, especially because our reading classes were getting so much larger. I realized that we needed a bigger building, but I wanted to create a real learning and training center where we could operate professionally. I started to look and there was a parcel of land adjacent to our house for sale, but it was not big enough. I settled for a 13,000-square-foot lot a half a mile from Maison Chance. The price was affordable, so I bought it.

As it happened, I'd shared my vision with friends from Maison Chance Switzerland and they had agreed to absorb the costs—a total of 32,000 US dollars. We made a first deposit at the end of 1999, and in early 2000 we closed the deal. The next step was to prepare a practical plan for the new building that we intended to call the "Take Wing Center."

*"Finally, I met a priest who worked both in the United Catholic Committee and as a Member of Parliament, a rare case in a socialist country."*

# CHAPTER 7

# A Second Partner

Our three-year "forced" partnership with the local Red Cross was coming to an end. Since I didn't want to extend it, I set about finding a new and hopefully more sympathetic partner. That was a tall order because a new partner would have to be either state-run or state-recognized and willing to affiliate with a foreign NGO. Among others, I approached the national Red Cross, the Health Service and the Youth League, but nothing worked out. Maison Chance had its own history and potential partners were either reluctant to come on board or they were out of sync with the kind of activities that we pursued.

Then I remembered a priest I had met years before at a church on Lê Văn Sỹ Street. He was in charge of the Ho Chi Minh City Catholic Solidarity Committee, one of a mere handful of Vietnamese NGOs. He was also known for his humanitarian outlook and for his success in becoming his church's representative in the National Assembly, a rare feat under a Communist regime. He was well aware of Maison Chance's activities and agreed to a five-year partnership with us so that we could continue to operate. I told him about our plans to expand the school and vocational center for the disadvantaged. He approved, and I drew up the contract.

## Hiệp Left Us

We signed the new partnership agreement on March 7, 2001, which was also the day we mourned the first death in our family. I was printing out the contract documents the night before when the hospital called to say that one of our residents, admitted the previous week with fever and high blood pressure, was in critical condition.

All 50 of us at Maison Chance quickly descended on the hospital. The doctors told us that Hiệp had suffered a debilitating brain haemorrhage and there was little more they could do. He'd been in a coma for days, kept alive by massive doses of medication but his pulse had been steadily growing weaker.

We stayed at the hospital, but I went home at midnight to put the finishing touches on the contract. At 6 a.m. the hospital informed us that Hiệp's breathing was growing increasingly labored. Clearly, the end was near.

It had not rained for some time but on the morning of March 7 the sun was shining brightly when a sudden shower drenched Saigon. Then, like a desert mirage, the rain stopped, just as Hiệp exhaled his final breath. I'd been looking after our family for seven years, and the sick never failed to recover. This was the first time a member of Maison Chance had died.

I'll never forget that day. In Vietnam, they say funerals bring luck. Hiệp left us on the day we signed the papers securing a future for Maison Chance. Surely, I thought, he must be our guardian angel.

## *The Priest's Assistant*

Our partnership with the Catholic priest got off to a good start; it was easier to deal with the priest than with the Red Cross. His organization took care of handicapped kids and sick people, just like Maison Chance, so we shared the same preoccupations. But he was a busy man, wearing many hats—Vice-President of the Catholic Solidarity Committee of Vườn Xoài Parish, Director of Thiên Phước Center for children with dioxin poisoning, and National Assembly representative. He was also overseeing many economic projects that he himself had spearheaded. Consequently, he had precious little time for Maison Chance, but he had total confidence in me. He readily signed any papers we needed and, as required by law, he sent his most loyal assistant to us as his on-site representative.

This person's job was to co-manage Maison Chance with me. She was in her fifties and, unlike the Red Cross representative, she was a hard worker. Her seriousness pleased me, even though I detected a kind of old-school severity about her. She was one of the first ever professional social workers in Vietnam, a devout Catholic who was single and dressed like a nun. I had high hopes that her strong sense of ethics and integrity would have a positive effect on Maison Chance.

There were now six of us in the cramped office and there was barely enough room to move around. Still, we bought a water cooler to accommodate the newcomer, who wanted it placed beside her desk.

The social worker was having difficulty interacting with some of the children, especially Thành. The teenager was certainly more grown-up, but still quite a character. In class, for example, he couldn't concentrate and constantly interrupted the other children, so much so that we had to organize special lessons just for his benefit. I realized that his dreadful childhood had scarred him for life and accepted the fact that he would never be completely normal. Besides, he was still receiving treatment for his heart and I prayed he would not require surgery.

## Little Monkey Thành

Thành liked cold water and could drink a gallon or more a day. He carried a big plastic container filled with ice wherever he went. He was obviously intrigued by the water cooler and came into the office several times a day to use it. This irked the social worker no end and she finally put her foot down. "The machine is off-limits. It's strictly reserved for 'important' people in the office," she declared. She accused Thành of spilling water on her papers and scolded him each time he approached the cooler.

Maison Chance's mission was to take care of people who previously had no access to education and to help them to overcome their difficulties. The priest's assistant, on the other hand, felt that our beneficiaries ought to be grateful and needed to show respect to their helpers. She thought they were ill-mannered, especially Thành. This teenager, who loved me, could not stand anyone who appeared to him to be rude and he would not hesitate to demonstrate his displeasure.

One morning, the social worker was inspecting the boys' quarters when she found a jar filled with excrement. She was livid, and all the more so when she discovered that Thành was the culprit. "It's from me," he said defiantly, "a special gift for you, Madame." Furious, she pulled the huge plastic water container off the cooler and threw it in his direction. It missed him by a hair.

A few months after that, another incident occurred. Returning from a European trip, I found out that the social worker had expelled

Hạnh, one of our disabled residents. When I asked her why, she explained that visitors to Maison Chance expected to see poor, needy people and therefore it wasn't possible to continue harboring a girl who wore makeup and jewelry. She also wondered out loud how on earth Hạnh could have afforded such luxuries.

Thành witnessed our discussion and intervened. "I was with Hạnh when she bought those earrings and they only cost 2,000 đồng (or roughly 14 US cents)," he said. "She just wants to look pretty. It's only normal, especially if you're a handicapped person." Turning to the social worker, he continued, "I'd suggest you stop going to Mass. It's no use pretending to be religious after you've so thoughtlessly dismissed a poor handicapped girl." That shut her up.

Thành always felt a strong bond with disadvantaged people. He often asked me to organize visits to the psychiatric ward where he used to live. "Those people are so unlucky," he said, "they don't have enough to eat, we must help them." Thanks to him we started a tradition; each Christmas season our big family would visit the 1,500 children in the Center, bringing them Christmas cheer and gifts. Thành played Santa Claus, perspiring under his red wool costume and long white beard.

*"Thanks to this whale of a bus, all members of Maison Chance could have a summer holiday on the beach."*

# CHAPTER 8

# *On the Road*

For the last three years, the number of residents at Maison Chance increased steadily. There were now about 50 people under our roof. The residents came from every part of the country, from the north to the south. They were of different ages and each of them had a different handicap to overcome, but they shared the same misfortune. Though they were not related to one another, their fate had brought them close together.

Everyone participated in the housekeeping chores. The physically disabled adults shared their life experiences with the young while the younger residents helped the handicapped with their personal needs. Everyone had a role and a responsibility in this new family.

## The Lambrettas

We used bicycles, wheelchairs and motor scooters for transportation. But group outings—for medical checkups or to the swimming pool, for example—were an altogether different affair. For several years now, we used to charter the Lambrettas, a kind of

*The Lambretta Motorcycle is the fusion of a motor bike and a small truck.*

motorized three-wheel pickup van, from one of the local grocers who lived in front of the village church. Lambrettas weren't exactly speedy but at least they were cheap and each Lambretta could take up to ten passengers. Mind you, the rides were rough and very noisy, and after each trip we all smelled of gasoline.

## The Henry Dunant Award

In 2001 the Geneva-based Henry Dunant Foundation, so named in honor of the founder of the Red Cross, voted to award its annual field prize to Maison Chance. Moreover, we were told that the award ceremony would be held in Vietnam as a public demonstration of my country's support for my work in Maison Chance Vietnam.

We spent a long time preparing for the event which was going to take place in the vacant lot adjacent to our house in Binh Hung Hoa. It was very convenient for us. However, on the day of the event, I was told that the police had refused us permission to hold the celebrations locally and that we had to quickly find an alternative venue in the Saigon city center. We booked the New World Hotel and then made travel arrangements for our guests to get to the city venue. The last-minute decision baffled me, and I could only assume that it had to do with the construction work along the two-mile dirt road leading to our village.

The award ceremony finally took place at the city venue, the five-star New World Hotel, on April 22, 2002 as scheduled. Guests arrived punctually and included the Swiss Ambassador and the Swiss Consul, the president of the Henry Dunant Foundation, Vietnamese government officials, the French Consul and his wife as well as friends and supporters of Maison Chance. But there was no sign of the hosts; the Maison Chance members were nowhere to be seen.

The rainy season, which came early that year, was to blame. The five Lambrettas arrived on time to fetch their 50 passengers. We proceeded to board everyone, loading the wheelchairs onto the vehicle roof. It was pouring rain and two of the vehicles refused to start, stranding 20 of us. The other three Lambrettas went ahead, slowing down at every turn so as not to tip over their roof cargo. When we finally made it to the New World Hotel, we were an hour late, soaking wet and embarrassed. Luckily for all concerned, in Vietnam, 'rubber time' was tolerated.

There was one final hurdle. The hotel's elevator system was out of order, forcing us to carry the more than 30 disabled guests from the lobby to the first-floor reception room. The assembled crowd looked on in amazement; it was quite a contrast to their luxurious and elegant surroundings!

## The Whale Bus

We used the Henry Dunant award money to buy a badly needed vehicle—a ten-year-old gray Toyota minibus, shipped directly from Japan. It had four rows of seats and could legally transport 15 passengers or fewer if we had to carry wheelchairs.

*The Henry Durant Award ceremony at New World Hotel Saigon in the presence of Swiss representatives to Vietnam. Six years later a group of extremist anti-Communist Vietnamese used this photograph to prove that I worked as a spy for the Vietnam Communist Party. (See CHAPTER 14)*

## *The Very First Holiday by the Sea*

Thanks to the Whale Bus, members of Maison Chance could enjoy a holiday by the sea for the very first time. We decided to spend ten days in Nha Trang, a resort city known for its scenic shores and sandy beaches, about 280 miles northeast of Saigon.

The problem was that everyone wanted to come along, and the bus could not take us all. After some negotiation, 15 members agreed to stay behind, either because they were unwell, busy with other things, or had been disciplined for bad behavior. Even then we still had to leave 35 people and we had no choice but to make two trips. I left with the first group. The bus was loaded to bursting, carrying 16 adults and children, their wheelchairs and luggage.

Our first stop was in the Central Highlands, where we hiked through coffee plantations and excitingly admired Dalat's famous waterfalls. We made another stop in Cà Ná, a small village down the coast famous for its turquoise waters and pretty seaside bungalows. We stayed there for a few days and cooked the local fishermen's mixed catch at dinner time.

Meanwhile, our driver returned to Saigon to fetch the second group. They went straight to Nha Trang where we eventually caught up with them at a hotel in Tran Quy Street. We slept four to a double bed but by the end everyone found a corner in which to rest.

So, we began ten days of fun and relaxation. For some, this was the first time they saw the sea and they were eager to learn to swim. Others lazed for hours on inflatable floats, going as far as the buoy that marked the limit of the swimming area. Someone even wrote "Maison Chance 070803" on the side of the buoy.

Immersed in the water, the disabled soon felt light and buoyant, as though their disabilities had temporarily disappeared. These memorable moments reminded us of how happy it is to be alive.

*On the beach in Nha Trang*

We made special friends with the local street kids who sold postcards, shined shoes, or picked up trash. Some of them went swimming with us and we took 20 of them back to the hotel where they could shower. We also offered them clean clothes. The parents of these kids worked in the fields in the north during the summer time and they had to leave their children to fend for themselves.

## Long, the Sprout of Faith

I noticed one boy whose name was Long and who had a different accent than the others. He told me he came from the highlands and had been living in Nha Trang for two weeks, picking up trash. He was only 15 and had never known his father. After his mother remarried, his stepfather had taken a dislike to him and thrown him out of the house. Ever since, he'd been wandering aimlessly. He would visit his mother from time to time until his stepfather caught him, beat him up and threatened to kill him if he dared come back. It was then that he ran away.

Long soon became a member of our group. Two days before the end of our stay, I put a question to him: "Do you want to come and live with us? You'll learn to read and write, to add and subtract, and you'll also learn a trade. You won't need to beg or pick up trash anymore." He gave me a great big smile and didn't sleep a wink the night before we set out for Maison Chance.

We came back from our vacation with one more child. Long was very intelligent and learned fast, and I thought he'd fit in our family nicely. But one evening I found him in my room rummaging through my armoire. I told him that stealing was simply not done and besides, there was no need to steal in order to survive at Maison Chance. He became frightened and ran away.

It was a long five years before I saw him again. He came back one day with his tail between his legs. He appeared to have done well in Saigon and said he had no wish to come back to Maison Chance. He just wanted to apologize for trying to steal, telling me he felt shame and regret for having betrayed my trust. That was a great consolation; something good had indeed emerged from the confidence I'd placed in him.

*"They'd never seen so many white faces and such big noses, or other people with black skins and colorful clothes."*

# CHAPTER 9

# *Friends from Overseas*

One person could hardly achieve good deeds single handed. If I wasn't willing to share the Maison Chance story with others around me, no one would have heard about us. So, I became a spokesperson for those destitute people we were helping. Besides starting a news bulletin in 1997, I returned to Europe every year to spread the good word and talk about our work to anyone who cared to hear about the plight of the children and the handicapped that had been left to their own devices in Vietnam.

On a visit to Geneva in 1996 I met a dynamic woman named Vivien Harris who deeply loved Vietnam. She in turn introduced me to a Vietnamese expatriate who'd been living in Switzerland for over three decades. Mr. Thịnh had just been named President of the Association for the Children of Vietnam.

Mr. Thịnh and his wife, Hương, had two sons, the elder of whom was my age. He had already left home, and I was offered his room whenever I was in town. I grew up in Geneva but hadn't lived there for a long time. Now, when I'm back in my country, my new home is with a Vietnamese family.

## The First Maison Chance Event in Europe

In 2001, in a parish lounge in Lausanne, Thịnh helped me organize my first Maison Chance evening. I donned an *áo dài* for the event. (The *áo dài*, a traditional Vietnamese dress, is a tight-fitting silk tunic worn over trousers. *Áo* translates as "shirt" and *Dài* means "long".)

In spite of the occasion, I felt a little self-conscious wearing such a traditional costume outside of Vietnam. I had it made to wear at Hiền's wedding, one of the young orphans I'd taken under my wing. This was only the second time I'd wore the tunic and I thought a pair of flashy earrings would match, but as the event was about to start I heard Hương's command, "Take them off, Tim, they're not really appropriate. Don't forget, you're here on behalf of the poor." I was grateful for the advice and immediately felt more at ease without earrings. I was still growing into my new role.

A hundred or so people showed up. I began narrating a video which I'd prepared ahead of time. As the pictures appeared on the screen, my thoughts and worries about my appearance vanished. I had an hour to deliver my message; just one evening to convey to our supporters the urgent needs of the most disadvantaged people in Vietnamese society. I was in my element; the words just came out of my mouth without my having to think about them.

## Training Abroad in France

After the event in Switzerland, I traveled to France at the invitation Maison Chance France. There, in the Rhône-Alpes Region's sister city of Ho Chi Minh City, I was able to spell out our needs for vocational training. The association began to support us in 1999 by helping Maison Chance to develop a painting workshop which created designs suitable for printing on textile, a specialisation of this region. First, a designer came to Vietnam to teach us basic techniques. Then, in 2001, two of our apprentices—a teenager and a young man in a wheelchair—were chosen for a two-month training program in Croix-Rousse, the famous hilltop city in Lyon which had been home to silk weavers and their looms since the 16th century.

I flew to France with my two boys, both of whom looked nervous before we took off. "Tim, I want to have a smoke," said one, "can you help me open the window?" And after we arrived in Lyon, they were astonished by what they saw—the dry air, the gray skies, vehicles and the people who were not at all like those at home. They'd never seen so many white faces with such big noses, or other people with black skins and colorful clothes, to say nothing of how tall some people were and how heavy! The boys had trouble getting used to the food; dairy products in particular. "Disgusting," they exclaimed, desperately yearning for a little plain boiled rice.

We were staying with some members of the association. Our two Asians did their best to follow Western customs and they meant well, but mishaps were inevitable. In the bathroom, for example, they discarded toilet paper in the trash bin because in Vietnam plumbing pipes were narrow and paper could clog the drains. The French found the practice less than hygienic. Electric stoves were another issue since the boys kept forgetting to turn them off after use. With gas, at least they could see the flame.

The two trainees loved eating kebabs at the lively Place des Terreaux at the foot of Croix-Rousse. It wasn't expensive, they explained, and the kebabs tasted far better than French food. One day I found them sitting at an outdoor café at Place Terreaux with a mischievous glint in their eyes. "We'll have a nice dinner tonight," they said proudly. I didn't understand at first, and then I saw something moving in their backpack. They had caught two pigeons and were now looking forward to a delectable feast. I explained that the birds were usually diseased, inedible and would likely be confiscated by the health department. "Release them," I urged. They were genuinely surprised by my reaction, and unconvinced.

That evening we met again at a handicapped friend's apartment which was specially adapted for wheelchair access. It was available for us for two weeks while the owner was out of town. The boys had already been there for more than an hour and I was famished. I opened the refrigerator and could scarcely believe what I saw: two birds dressed and ready for the pot.

## Thoughts on Architectural Design for the Project and the Last Decision

While in Europe my thoughts were constantly on the progress of the Take Wing Center Project, which was supported by Maison Chance France. An architect friend of mine in Paris drew up the first design for this future training and education center. We had sat through long meetings in Lyon and Paris in an attempt to clearly define the function for each area of the new building.

Initially we planned to have only one floor. The architect proposed a futuristic concept using polycarbonate, a transparent material similar to glass only more shatter-resistant. Our goal was to bring natural light into the building. Next, a model was built and dispatched first to Lyon and then to Geneva in order to introduce the concept to our potential sponsors. We were worried that this model did not reflect the practicality of the space. Also, there was no assurance that the transparent panels could withstand the soaring temperatures and torrential tropical rains in southern Vietnam.

We seemed to be stuck at this point without any definite resolution.

To tell the truth, I only dreamt of a building with a tiled roof to fit into the traditional local style.

After discussions of pros and cons, we reverted to the plan with a structure better adapted to the climate, the local construction style and our modest budget. The challenge now was to find a builder who was able to meet our criteria and expectations. I had just returned from Europe when I received a phone call from a Mrs. Trang, the owner of a local construction company. She'd heard about Maison Chance on the news. She was enthusiastic about our project and offered her own services.

Association Maison Chance France was involved in the Take Wing Center project right from the beginning. They strongly emphasized the need to maintain transparency in management and financial matters in order to comply with the benefactor's requirements. We issued a call for bids and received a total of 20 in the end. Mrs. Trang's was the most professional, but I decided to visit the construction sites of the other bidders. I found cracks in walls, rooms improperly ventilated, and electric wires hanging about dangerously. Finally, I had a meeting with Mrs. Trang and she showed me examples of the work done by her company. Everything looked neat and clean and her workmen displayed high-quality craftsmanship. Her price was good, too. We signed our contract and work began immediately.

*"Our two French guests had an opportunity to taste one of our local delicacies: coconut larvae freshly harvested from the coconut-tree."*

# CHAPTER 10

## *Volunteers*

My first computer was instrumental in modernizing our bookkeeping system. I was able to write letters and create and print out charts and tables with just a few clicks! However, without an Internet connection, I still had to rely on the telephone, postal service and fax machines to communicate with the outside world. All that changed in 1999 when electronic mail became available at Maison Chance. Our address must have been listed on the Internet somehow because I started to receive many emails from people I didn't even know but who were interested in Maison Chance. This new means of communication was a big change for me. I could now instantly reach and interact with interested sponsors thousands of miles away.

By mid-2002, email became my main tool and the fastest way to keep in touch with our supporters. I received so many emails that sometimes could not respond fast enough.

### Clara and Fanfan

In the middle of that year, a young French woman named Clara, who was planning to travel in Vietnam with her boyfriend, wrote to me. Her email sat in my inbox for three weeks before I could respond to her. She rang me back straight away saying she and her companion, both 25, were planning a trip to Southeast Asia. They hoped to be more than just tourists; they wished to volunteer their time to some charities in the region. So as soon as they arrived in Vietnam they wrote to a number of charities run by the French here, but their good will offer was not readily accepted due to red tape. Everywhere they went, they were asked to provide detailed references, none of which, of course, they possessed.

My email therefore cheered Clara up. She wrote asking why there was such a fuss in accepting help. She said her partner Francois (nicknamed Fanfan) was so depressed by their numerous rejections that he insisted on changing their air ticket to return to France immediately. I made arrangements to meet them at Maison Chance the next day.

I accepted their offer, but I could not provide them any accommodations; we were completely full and in addition we were not legally allowed to offer lodging to foreigners at that time. There was no hotel in the area yet, but we managed to find them a small guesthouse next to the cemetery. They were the first foreigners ever to rent a room in the neighborhood and so they became instant celebrities! They walked to Maison Chance every morning and discovered their favourite breakfast food, Vietnamese sponge cake, from a street vendor. And they in turn became her favourite customers from Maison Chance.

Clara, a lawyer by training, took over the French class while Fanfan, an IT engineer, took charge of the computer room. Soon, Fanfan had an internal communications system set up and running. It linked the computer room, the office in the back and my upstairs office; a real revolution in communications in Vietnam at that time.

Clara was a dynamic teacher, and her classes were far less formal than those of her Vietnamese predecessor. More students enrolled in her class. She taught us to sing her favourite song "San Francisco." The words of the song, "On a hill sits a blue house. You can walk there, and no one has to knock on the door, the inhabitants there lost the keys a long time ago" aptly described Maison Chance.

## *A Trip to the Mekong Delta*

I invited Clara and Fanfan to join the Maison Chance residents on our annual summer holiday at Sóc Trăng Province. It was a good chance for the visitors to discover rural Vietnam. Sóc Trăng Province was an isolated location without electricity and it took us a day on the bus, a boat and a dinghy to get there. During the summer holiday for the previous few years, I had taken my orphaned children and the disabled residents there; they took turns each year to join in the holiday.

Tai's parents were our hosts. Tai had been living at Maison Chance for a while. His parents were both elderly and they lived in a small thatched hut in the middle of the Mekong Delta, reachable only by small dinghy.

We set out from Saigon at the crack of dawn and after a day of travelling everyone was tired, especially the two disabled residents in wheelchairs. After a few hours in the wooden boat, we finished the journey in a small dinghy which made slow progress on the river choked with river vegetation. We had a hard time pushing away the riverweeds while balancing our ten bodies, our baggage and the two wheelchairs in the small boat. The water was just up to the edge of the dinghy and some slipped in every time someone moved. Then someone had to bail the water out with a plastic cup.

It was dark by the time we caught sight of Tài's mother standing by the landing where we all clambered ashore. We stayed there for three days on the bank of the canal lined with sugar canes swaying gently

*Smiling Clara Ribeiro in her French class*

under the bright full moon as giant flocks of fireflies fluttering over the moonlit silvery water. We thought we were lost in the Milky Way.

The hut was on an islet in the middle of the rice paddies. As usual, Tài's parents were happy to see us and, although they were poor, they still managed to provide genuine hospitality. Our two French guests had an opportunity to taste one of our local delicacies: tasty coconut larvae freshly harvested from the coconut-tree. You could eat them raw or cooked in rice porridge. We were also offered sour fish soup with fresh fish from the nearby pond and some grilled field mice which the children had caught with the aid of their pocket flashlights. But while we ate our fill the mosquitoes enjoyed sucking our delicious blood.

Being an old hand at visiting, I knew how to deal with mosquitoes; I protected myself safely inside a large rice bag. Fanfan and Clara slept on a bamboo bed protected by a mosquito net. We told them not to let any part of their bodies touch the net. However, morning came, and he told me in French: "I've counted forty-nine mosquito bites on my backside." I thought that was funny and immediately translated it into Vietnamese. Our illiterate but diplomatic hosts knew better than to laugh at the remark. Such intimate details were simply not aired in public.

After three days, we returned to Saigon, stopping at the Phung Hiep floating market on the Mekong River. We could not resist the ducklings, so we bought three of them: one yellow, one white with a crest and another white one with some brown spots.

The ducklings suffered a bit on the way home but they all got back to Maison Chance in one piece. They settled into my room, but they were not easy to toilet train. They were constantly leaving their droppings every few steps and I spent a lot of time cleaning up after them.

When I cleaned the house, I took the ducks out to the roof yard where I hung my washing. After scrubbing them, I let the ducks back into the house. The first day one duckling disappeared and the next day another duckling went missing. I realized the giant rats living in the rooftop had feasted on my ducklings.

The French volunteers stayed with us for three months. One afternoon Clara came to see me, but she looked a bit pale and nauseated and generally not well. I took her to see the doctor and discovered that Clara and Fanfan were having a baby. The baby had been conceived in the guest house next to the cemetery. It would be a baby girl and Clara named her Tram after a student in her French class.

## Friends from France, Switzerland and Luxembourg

In early 2004, I received an email from a Frenchwoman who specialized in teaching French as a second language to foreigners and she was offering to help. I accepted her proposal without hesitation since she had the right qualifications. She took charge of our French class and was soon making rapid progress with her highly individual teaching methods despite being unable to understand a word of Vietnamese herself. She was extremely dynamic and committed to our goals. By the end of her stay, she had grown attached to our large family and was sad at the prospect of leaving us. And indeed, she didn't entirely leave us behind. Once back in France, she accepted the position of Secretary for Maison Chance France, so she's still part of the team.

The third French teacher at Maison Chance was Julien. He was French with Vietnamese blood in his veins. His father was part Vietnamese, but he was also deaf, so he couldn't teach Vietnamese to his own children. To understand his heritage, Julien majored in Vietnam's history and learned the language at a prestigious school in Paris. By the time he came to Maison Chance, he'd already acquired a solid background knowledge concerning Vietnam. Calm and accommodating, he was, like Clara, keen on spicing up his lessons with French songs. His favourite song was Jacques Brel's "Ne me quitte pas" or "Do not leave me."

Hát, my wheelchair-bound assistant was one of Julien's best students. Hát had a natural gift for communications and one of his responsibilities was to liaise with volunteers from abroad. Hát had overcome his handicap during his stay at Maison Chance. In 2002, he married a beautiful healthy lady and they moved out. I then hired and trained him as an accountant. He was among Maison Chance's first beneficiaries to have gained their independence. I felt proud of him, but I worried about his health. He worked hard, and I noticed that he was gradually growing weaker, though he always said he was feeling fine.

Like every year, I returned to Europe to maintain my contact with my supporters and to report on the progress of the Take Wing Center project. And like every year, all the residents of Maison Chance were standing at the front gate to see me off. I noticed that Hát had some difficulty in breathing and I knew he was not very well. I told him to stop working and go to see the doctor. Feeling very sad, I held him in my arms to say goodbye.

In France, I had maintained a solid contact in the Rhône-Alpes Region whose director, Mrs. Anne-Marie Comparini, had visited Maison Chance. She had agreed to financially support the operational cost of the Take Wing Center over a three-year period, just the kind of financial security we needed to round out our training programs.

In Luxembourg, the Lions Club and the Ministry of Foreign Affairs had agreed to contribute to the construction costs of the training center.

I also needed to catch up with my contacts at Bale, Switzerland in the German speaking Canton. One contact was Tina, the mother of a child with cerebral palsy who came to see us in Vietnam. When she returned home, she managed to collect 40 wheelchairs from various donors for Maison Chance.

My other contact was Luciano Pellegrini, president of the Basaid Association, a charity organization whose members were mainly from the company Novartis. He undertook to have the wheelchairs shipped to Vietnam by container ship.

Fluent in French, Italian and German, Luciano had sent one of the first containers of medical supplies to Vietnam in 1993, and since then he'd maintained a close relationship with this country. With him I could share everything, including the same concepts about love and marriage, and I will never forget what he once confided to me, "Love is like the cherry on the cake."

While I was with my friend Tina in Bale, only a week after I left Vietnam, I got a phone call from Vietnam. Hát had breathed his last breath.

Julien, our French and Vietnamese French teacher, had stayed with Hát, my faithful assistant, from the beginning till the end. Julien participated in the life of our big family and, without much choice, he became a member of Maison Chance.

It was the end of the year and time for the 2004 bookkeeping, but our books were in a sorry state because by the end Hát was so ill that he could not focus on his work. When I got back, I asked Julien to help out and finish up what Hát left behind. Julien accepted the task and with his assistance we managed to finalize our 2004 accounts.

After returning to Paris, Julien continued to support us. He became the treasurer of Maison Chance France. The association was founded in 1997 but it wasn't until eight years later that we organized its first public event in Lyon.

For this occasion, I brought Duy, a disabled member who required a wheelchair to France with me. Duy was learning the French language and he had traveled a long distance to talk about his life journey.

The gala event was organized by none other than Clara, Julien and France.

*"When it came to my turn to say some words, I could not utter a single word. I had made many speeches in front of any crowd previously, but that day I could only express my happiness through my tears. My feeling was intense."*

# CHAPTER 11

# The Take Wing Center

The Take Wing Center project began to fulfill its two main purposes: the first was to try to help as many of the poorest, most suffering people as possible and the second was to provide training based on the best of their abilities.

At that time, our school had only four small classrooms and so there was not enough space to teach writing and reading to both children from Maison Chance as well as the poor local children. Therefore, we had to enlarge the classrooms.

Maison Chance was by then a home, a school, and a clinic as well as several training workshops. All the activities of the residents took place in the same area and it was overcrowded. It was practically impossible to maintain any rules or regulations.

In the morning, the kids rolled out of bed to go to school, which was just underneath their bedroom. At break time some crawled back to bed again. The disabled residents were not used to any discipline so as soon as they entered the classroom; they wanted to go to the toilet. Of course, they would not be seen until lunch time; they hid in the kitchen or went back to their beds which were right next to the classroom. It was easy indeed to play truant.

The Take Wing Center would be a good answer to both problems.

All Maison Chance residents had to go to school, therefore the distinction between school and home was clearer and at the same time we could double the size of our classrooms to meet the demand from the local poverty-stricken community.

The Center would be built on the block of land which we had recently bought of just less than 14,000 square yards. It was a little less than a mile from the house. We would move all educational activities and vocational training to the new premises.

Working drawings for the project had been done thanks to the cooperation of the company Nam Thien Loc owned by Mrs. Trang and her husband, Mr. Trung, who was also an architect. They were very professional and trustworthy. We signed a contract for this project with them.

According to the drawing, the Center would have five large classrooms for basic learning, four rooms for vocational training, a large office, a clinic, a reception area and a product display room.

We planned to include three separate rooms for volunteers from abroad plus a canteen with a kitchen attached.

There would be ramp for wheelchair access between two floors.

## *Fund Raising and Application for the Building Permit*

To raise enough money to finance this project, I had to ask for help from a lot of people. From 2000 to 2004 I went fund raising in

Switzerland, France, Belgium, Luxembourg and the United States by presenting my Take Wing Center project.

The initial sponsors required that I have the local building permit first before they made their decision. Meanwhile, the Vietnamese authorities demanded that I prove Maison Chance had enough money to cover the cost of the project before they could issue a permit. And the estimate cost for the project had gone up to over 350,000 US dollars.

I then decided to ask all my possible donors just to put down the sums of money they wished to contribute. Letters went back and forth and, except a few who still insisted on building permit first, I got enough support.

By May 2005, we got the building permit.

We had to start building immediately; the wet season was upon us. Mrs. Trang consulted the calendar for a good day to start. May 17 turned out to be a good day, so we started preparations to begin the project; it was only a short time from now to the good day.

## *The Project Begins*

More than 150 guests attended the laying of the foundation stone ceremony. To appease God to bless the project, the adults offered burning incense and a roasted suckling pig while the children performed the lion dance on the cleared construction land.

A priest representing the United Catholic Association in Ho Chi Minh City was the keynote speaker. I chatted with guests, met our new neighbors and encouraged the project's workers. To conclude the ceremony, I invited all the guests back to Maison Chance for light refreshments.

For this occasion, Mrs. Trang and her husband Mr. Trung brought along a friend, Mr. Pham Hong Ky, to meet me after the ceremony. Mr.

*The Take Wing Center with its blue walls and red roof.*
*It was located in the fields.*

Ky, who was formerly head of the Vietnam's Department of Planning and Investment for the South, also spent many years working in Germany. He enjoyed our chat and invited me to have a ride on his 1970 motor car. He seemed to be a joyful and honest man. We like each other instantly.

At the light lunch the Priest produced a bottle of whiskey and offered me a small glass, but I had to decline; it was in the middle of a hot day. Now I could relax and enjoy myself.

The project started along with the rains.

The builders tried to excavate the soil for the foundation, but as soon as the hole was dug it was filled with the next rain water. They had to use heavy duty pumps to remove the water as much as possible. However, as soon as the water was pumped out, another downpour refilled the pit, so they had to start again and again.

Into the second week of the construction, Mrs. Trang politely asked me if I could clear the first invoice.

I knew the bill needed to be paid, but I also realized that as the foundation stone was laid, I had only a bundle of promissory notes in my hands; my bank account was still empty.

I immediately telephoned Mr. Luciano Pellegrini, chairman of BASAID at Bale. This generous, big-hearted person was the largest contributor to the Take Wing Center project. He was my trusted supporter and friend. He immediately transferred his donation, and soon after other donations arrived. The construction of Take Wing Center proceeded according to plan.

## The Opening Ceremony of Take Wing Center

After nine months of work, my dream of the Take Wing Center had come true.

The Center was opened on the February 18, 2006 in the presence of over 200 guests including the chairman of the People's Committee of Ho Chi Minh City and the honorable consul of Switzerland. My friend Luciano Pellegrini and his colleague Simon Rey also attended as they came early from far away Switzerland to help us prepare for the opening.

When it came to my turn to make a statement, I could not utter a word. I had made many speeches in front of large crowds before, but that day I could only express my happiness through my tears. My feeling was intense.

*The opening of the Take Wing Center on February 18, 2006.*

*"Students are admitted to Maison Chance
School for free under one of the three following
conditions:
They are too old to go to normal public schools,
They lack the identity papers or a birth
certificate required to be admitted to normal
public schools, or
They are too poor to pay the school fee."*

*Wheelchair riders at the entrance of the Take Wing Center.*

# CHAPTER 12

# Between Two Places

The distance between Maison Chance and the Take Wing Center is just under a mile; a fair distance for wheelchair users to go back and forth several times daily.

Of course, our bus was the fastest means of transport to shuttle the disabled, especially the quadriplegics who could not manage by themselves on the bumpy road.

During the wet season, the road to the Take Wing Center was not usable since it was lined with puddles and potholes. And since the last 440 yards was unpaved, the mud stuck to the wheels of the chairs and made pushing them impossible for the children trying to help the disabled. They all looked miserable when arrived at the Center. Since the authorities did not have any plans to seal the road we decided to cement the last 400 plus yards of the long road ourselves.

Now we could use the road all year round so we bought bicycles for the kids and wheelchairs for the disabled and they could immediately manage by themselves much faster.

## Twice as Crowded

Besides the three rooms used for painting, sewing and computing which were transferred over from Maison Chance, we added a room at the Take Wing Center for woodworking in which we tried to manufacture products made with bamboo. The woodworking room was used as a testing place for students who were not sure about their vocation or for those who were not suitable for other courses which we offered.

Students are admitted to Maison Chance School for free under one of the three following conditions:

They are too old to go to normal public schools,

They lack the identity papers or a birth certificate required to be admitted to normal public schools, or

They are too poor to pay school fee.

We also established a library with a collection of books on different subjects suitable to the needs of the schoolchildren; the world of books was completely new for the students from this poverty-stricken community. They loved looking at picture books. Through the books we could introduce culture to the children; however we met with some difficulty here.

The parents of the poor children did not appreciate the power of books. After school, they would rather see their kids selling lottery tickets or doing something which they reckoned more fruitful than reading books. We therefore felt the need to have a 'parents and teachers meeting' to explain to them the importance of reading and education. The mothers and fathers had to assist us in educating the children so that their families could have a brighter future.

At the beginning of 2006, there were 170 primary school children, 65 disabled individuals in vocational training and a staff of 30. Our workload was doubled.

At lunchtime, the kitchen prepared and cooked meals for 265 persons and the canteen overflowed with diners. Sometimes children and individuals in wheelchairs took over the entrance lobby as well.

The upkeep cost of the Take Wing Center increased daily.

In 2006, the expenditure exceeded 160,000 US dollars annually. This sum covered the food, the caring for all residents, wages for the staff, maintenance cost and other cost associated with current projects.

## *Vincent and the Development of Product Manufacture*

For the last two years Vincent Cormier, a French volunteer, had been managing the vocational training courses at Maison Chance. Vincent continued this duty at the Take Wing Center.

Vincent Cormier was an important person in my life. Four months younger than me, he was French with a Canadian passport. He loved journalism but like a good son he listened to his parent's advice and followed the path that they chose for him. He lived in Canada for five years, then came to discover new horizons in Vietnam. Soon he landed a job teaching French at the French Cultural Center in Saigon (IDECAF)

He visited at Maison Chance one nice day in October 2003 and offered his help.

In the beginning, I asked him to work with Hát, my accountant assistant, to help us check over our international accounts.

Afterwards, he looked at the training and manufacturing programs for us since he had some experience in these fields.

Finally, he took over the operation of the training and manufacturing completely. Vincent was a great help for us in setting a high standard in production for us to follow.

For me, Vincent was an outstanding collaborator. I shared with him every aspect of Maison Chance, from internal organisation to international affairs. At this point Vincent was one of the few who had the most complete knowledge and understanding the works of Maison Chance, and by that time I already had so many ideas for my

*The entire Maison Chance family photographed at the Take Wing Center in 2007.*

future projects. I dreamt of a village suitable for disable access and a Maison Chance in the country side. Vincent was trustworthy, and he was my best and only official advisor.

Vincent, like Lady Michelham and Mr. Luciano Pellegrini, were the people that had influenced me in my choice of the management style of this organization. These three people had given me very valuable advice; they were all thinking with their intelligent hearts.

Besides selling our products to other Maison Chance Associations around the world, we also had a few other commercial outlets for the handicraft we produced to sell overseas.

Terre des Hommes in Alsace was our first distributor. At that time Mrs. Brigitte Hammen was in charge of the association operations in Vietnam. She paid us a visit early in 1997 when we were busy building, however she appreciated our efforts and so Terre des Hommes became our first partner.

Mr. Luciano of BASAID gave us a large order. Every year when I

*The Sewing Room*

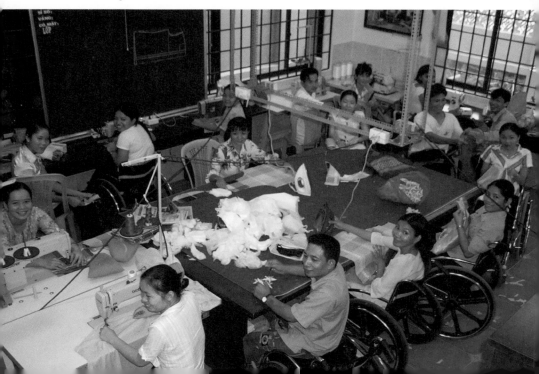

visited Europe I always stopped at Bale to see Luciano and his wife, Tina. He gave me ideas for new products preferred by local consumers.

Once when I was at Bale, Tina received a box containing 500 key holders with little cotton mice attached,which we made in our sewing room. Tina was looking forward to selling them at the Christmas Fair; however this particular box of goods presented a big problem. The key rings and the stuffed mice were not connected but were in separate bags. The Maison Chance people in charge of this product did not finish their job properly and it took Tina and her assistant a long time to attach the key rings to the mice. They were not happy.

Luciano was also not pleased, and he told me that I was not professional. I said it was not my fault, but Luciano said the products came from Maison Chance, so it was I who was ultimately responsible. I realized that he was right. I apologized, and I had learned a good lesson.

Mrs. Weber, who worked for the Swiss Consulate in South Vietnam, was also a valuable partner. She was dedicated to the caring of the poor here. Mrs. Weber introduced us to the WWF (World Wide Fund) in Switzerland and as a result we got an annual order for colorful stars in purple boxes. We signed a contract to supply this product for four years. WWF bought our products to give them away as their Christmas gifts. So over 25,000 stars made by Maison Chance would decorate thousands of homes in Switzerland for Christmas.

After over four years working at Maison Chance, Vincent told me he would slowly extricate himself from Maison Chance to follow another calling—the calling of Jesus Christ. I was surprised because I had never heard Vincent mention any religion and sometimes he even joked about my 'spiritual life'.

I was sad trying to argue my case that helping the unfortunate residents at Maison Chance was also like doing Christ's work. But Vincent desired to return to France to study theology and finally I had to let him follow his heart.

*"To respond to the demand for suitable accommodations for the handicapped, I had to put my thinking cap on.*
*I began thinking about the third project: VILLAGE CHANCE, the Lucky Village. I wanted to construct an apartment building suitable for the handicapped that was completely wheelchair accessible."*

# CHAPTER 13

# The Road to Independence

The contract we had signed with the United Catholic Association in Ho Chi Minh City as our local partner was nearly expired, so we had to look for a new local partner. Mrs. Trang, the assistant director for the construction company Nam Thien Loc and now a friend of mine, suggested that I contact Mr. Ky. I had met him at the ceremony to lay the foundation stone for the Take Wing Center and I liked Mr. Ky a lot.

I agreed with Mrs. Trang's suggestion and I met Mr. Ky at a café bar near the airport chosen by my friend. The special menu included brown beer, German sausages, and Russian-style smoked cheese; all delicacies from Germany and other Central European countries where Mr. Ky spent a few years working in foreign affairs.

Our conversation was all about the future development of Maison Chance, how to maintain it for a long time and what the best logical way to get it approved, officially and legally, was.

Our organisation is quite unique; we are not the same as any other NGOs which usually provide funds for a project carried out by its local partner. These projects typically lasted from one to five years and after that the sponsoring NGO would withdraw and the project would end.

The projects of Maison Chance were totally different from the other NGO endeavours.

Maison Chance was founded in Vietnam by one person and I sought to build Maison Chance on a solid foundation so that it would last. I did not wish to temporarily lean on a local partner. Maison Chance's mission was not limited by a certain period of time. Maison Chance needed a secured legal foundation so its future and the future of its members who depended on our services were guaranteed.

I knew of a road that would lead to this independence; I would become a Vietnamese citizen and apply with the Vietnamese Internal Affairs authorities for permission to found Maison Chance as a Vietnamese NGO.

Mr. Ky enjoyed drinking his German beer in a yard glass, gently nodding his head. He liked my idea, but he reckoned it would take a long time and he had a simpler, temporary solution.

He knew the Association for Helping Unfortunate Patients, a Vietnamese NGO sponsored by retired elders who used to be in the army and were of social importance. He suggested that this Vietnamese NGO would be our new local partner and at the same time we would become one of its branches. This would allow us to maintain our independent management of Maison Chance and at the same time become a part of the local NGO for our legal status.

The Association for Helping Unfortunate Patients did not allow a foreigner to sit on their Management Committee, so we decided to elect Mr. Ky as the Chairperson of the new branch and I would be the Vice Chairperson.

In January 2007, the President and Founder of the Association for Helping Unfortunate Patients signed the order to establish Maison Chance as a new branch member.

The President, formerly the Chairman of the People's Committee of Ho Chi Minh City, retired but he continued working. He established the first free hospital in Saigon and now he trusted me, a foreigner, to hold a position in a social services association of reconstructed Vietnam. I was so happy to be trusted by the chairman.

The negotiations and paper work relating to change in Maison Chance's status required a lot of time. The contract executed with the new local partner was not signed until May 2009 and it allowed Maison Chance to operate legally for the next five years.

The new page was turned. Now I could turn my attention to the people about whom I care and love.

## *Rejoining Society*

I loved to see my children happy. I worked to make their lives meaningful for the community. My ideal aim was to help my children and the disabled to be able to help themselves so that one day they could leave Maison Chance to free up the space for other unfortunate people. But it was not that simple in reality. For the serious paraplegic patients, to find a job in the outside world was practically impossible. Therefore, we had to create jobs for them at the Take Wing Center itself.

To prepare for an independent life, our paraplegic residents were first trained and when they participated in the manufacturing of products they were paid a basic salary. During this transitional period, they were required to set some money aside. At the end of the month, the residents of Maison Chance receive only 20 percent of their salary while the other 80 percent was deposited in a saving account in their own name but managed temporarily by Maison Chance.

This savings would be the means for them to later "take wing".

One of the first weddings celebrated at Maison Chance was the marriage of Hien, a disabled orphan, with a staff member caring for the serious paraplegic patients. They had met at our home.

The bride and groom registered their marriage application with the local People's Committee and the wedding was celebrated at home with a feast. The person in charge of the ceremony was chosen from the most respected senior members of the family. Like other orphans, Hien had no one to help so I volunteered to be Hien's next of kin.

The young couple rented a small place near Maison Chance which measured only 215 square feet. The home lacked windows and was always under water when it rained. In 2006 there were other couples who followed in Hien's steps, flying off their nest. Most of them ended up renting next to Hien. The closeness of their houses to Maison Chance was very convenient for the couples who had left Maison Chance. Since their rented place was not wheelchair accessible, most of them returned to Maison Chance daily for their personal hygiene.

Others rented near the Take Wing Center where they worked. Like any other people after a day at work, they just want to go home, clean up and rest. But their new life at rented houses was not that easy. These rented accommodations did not have any facilities for the disabled with wheelchairs.

Around us, the village of Binh Hung Hoa was experiencing a booming time, exploding with development as new houses mushroomed up out of old rice fields and water spinach ponds. The roads were being built and every time it rained they turned into large puddles. Due to the low-lying land here, everyone decided to raise their land up another meter above the road, and so it was necessary for every house to have steps at the entrance with a ramp for vehicles, especially wheelchairs. The ramps were too steep for wheelchairs and without help the disabled could not function on their own. In the wider society outside of Maison Chance, the disabled were not able to join in as I had expected.

## *Project Village Chance, the Lucky Village*

To respond to the demand for suitable accommodations for the handicapped, I had to put my thinking cap on.

I began thinking about the third project Village Chance, or the Lucky Village.

I wanted to construct an apartment building suitable for the handicapped that was completely wheelchair accessible;

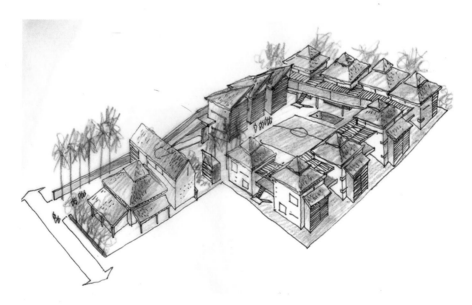

*The first sketch of Village Chance, one floor with thatched roof.*

new lodgings where a family with disabled members could live independently.

The price of land increased steadily, and we had to look hard to find a large piece of property for the third establishment.

A bit over half a mile away from the Take Wing Center, there was a big block of vacant land of nearly 38,000 square feet and the price was the lowest in the area.

It was July 2007 and the Village Chance project had been in my head for the last few months. Now I was ready to document the plan and present it to our sponsors. I had no concrete evidence of anything but a plan to buy this piece of land. I had to convince my benefactors with the value of all my ideas for the new project.

Right then something amazing happened. As I opened my email inbox, I thought something had gone wrong; hundreds of emails poured in nonstop. They were from overseas Vietnamese thanking us for our work in Vietnam and offering their help and support. This email phenomenon went on for a week before I found out the reason. A young Vietnamese computer wizard had reposted a television program featuring Maison Chance on YouTube, thereby introducing us to people all over the world.

Now back to the block of land which I wanted to buy to build the new Village Chance. I needed to finalize its purchase as soon as possible before the owner changed her mind or the price increased. I negotiated to buy it if the owner would let me pay it off within a year. We signed the contract in August 2007 and I guaranteed that I would have 480,000 US dollars to pay for the land on time.

*The surface area plan of Village Chance in square meter parcels showing the parcels of land bought by different sponsors. The largest parcels were bought by Michelham (887 square meters), The Mosikini Association (700 square meters) and 448 square meters bought by hundreds of Vietnamese residents in the US as a result of my last visit to California in September 2007.*

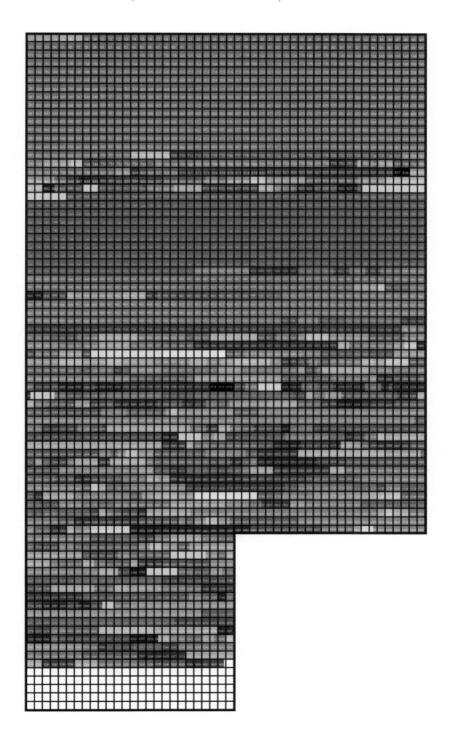

So, I had one year to raise this gigantic amount of money. The race against the clock had begun.

During this time my friend Vincent was preparing to leave Vietnam, but before departing for Rome he gave me an excellent idea.

We were buying over 3,500 square meters of land (or more than 4,100 square feet) so why didn't we cut the entire parcel into one square meter portions and alert our sponsors that they could buy as many one square meter parcels as they could afford.

The price of the land was enormous but when we divided it up into smaller portions the affordable amount to individual buyers looked more possible.

We received so many offers to purchase the square meters.

We drew up a plan with 3,500 squares and each time anyone bought a square, it would be colored in so that everyone could see what they had bought.

## A Visit to Little Saigon, California

One of the emails to arrive after the YouTube video came from Trung. A single man, he lived happily in North California. Trung emailed me daily and he had already bought a few wheelchairs for us and he sent me photographs of them for my approval. He had even sat in one to get it from inside the house to the street to test the quality of the chair. He also proposed to buy over 20 paintings from the disabled artists to sell by himself in California.

Besides Trung, the entertainment company "Paris by Night in the United States" also was aware of Maison Chance and they invited me to Southern California to participate in the program entitled "Portraits of Vietnamese Women." I appeared with two other women; a Vietnamese Buddhist nun and a Christian sister. The program was to be presented at the Theatre of Long Beach in a magnificent room occupied by over 3,000 guests. The show was recorded on DVD and it was shown everywhere in the world where there were any Vietnamese residents.

I let Trung know the good news and I promised to bring along the paintings which he had ordered.

Trung decided to come to meet me in Southern California and to hand over the wheelchairs as well, so we met in Little Saigon as planned. Trung was an easy going, happy person. We understood each other as soon as we met for the first time and I thought of Trung as my elder brother.

I originally planned to stay there only three days, but I ended up staying for two weeks. After my presentation, the chairperson of the Vietnamese Student's Association proposed a function to raise funds for Maison Chance. The gathering took place at the Paracel restaurant. It quickly filled up and we ran out of seats, so a lot of guests had to stand up. Over 500 people turned up to find out more about Maison Chance and all the paintings Trung had bought were auctioned off.

During the extra, unplanned time in California, Trung drove me everywhere from one interview to the next and he acted as my secretary as well. I met lot of people on the trip, so he compiled a list of the names of hundreds of new friends of Maison Chance in the US.

A Vietnamese business man let me use one of his rooms in his powdered milk store. At night the store was locked I had to climb over the fence to get in. In the morning, I saw a dozen Mexican laborers loading powdered milk into his truck. They were illegal laborers without papers and they slept overnight elsewhere. They all smiled when they saw me coming out from the room.

After 10 days in the United States, I had raised a lot of money and Trung was worried that I kept so much cash in the unsecured room. I had overlooked this matter, so listened to Trung's advice. We counted the money and then had it transferred to Vietnam. It was over 65,000 US dollars.

## The Trip to Mexico

Forty-eight hours before returning to Vietnam, I asked Trung "Where do the poor live?" He told me that there were not many in Southern California but if I went to Mexico I would find some people a bit like in Vietnam. So, I asked him if I could visit Mexico and he agreed to take me. The afternoon after the last interview we were on the freeway heading toward Mexico. At the border we were asked to pay 250 US dollars for insurance. Our car had no value in their country but without the payment we would have had to stay overnight at the border. So, we returned to the US to sort out the insurance and did not cross the border until the next morning.

Once we were in Mexico, everything was different; "Clean California" was in the past. We kept driving straight forward and the surrounding landscape was mainly bare brown and gray hills.

We drove to Ensenada, a small-town northwest of Mexico City on the Pacific Ocean coast. We chatted with some local people. Their simplicity and happiness reminded me of Vietnam. I suggested we go and visit the cathedral in the city. Trung was surprised at the request and he said, "Why the cathedral? I thought I was the religious person." I replied that even if I did not adhere to a religion, which did not mean I did not have any faith.

All religions teach love and I also believe in love. When we got to the cathedral, there were a dozen people praying behind the stone walls. I noticed a young man deep in prayer. We sat meditating for a while and when I was leaving I turned around and realized there was a large tumour behind his ear.

We stayed overnight in Mexico and then drove back in time for my flight from Los Angeles airport. At the border we were stopped by a female police officer and we ended up having to give her our last dollars to get out of Mexico. Luckily, I was on time for my flight.

Trung and I had time to have long conversation during this trip. We talked about many things but mainly about the formation of Maison Chance in the United States. Trung agreed to follow up on this program.

Back in Vietnam, I continued to talk to Trung and to new members to form a Maison Chance in the US. We decided to use Trung's address at Sacramento, the capital of California, to be the address of Maison Chance USA.

## The Visit of the Minister for Finance of the Federation of Switzerland

That same year, Mrs. Doris Leuthardt, Federation Consultant and Minister for Finance of the Federation of Switzerland, visited us. First, she visited our Vietnam Maison Chance with a delegation from Foreign Affairs as well as company directors and bankers. After a brief tour of our home, I took a ride with Mrs. Leuthardt in her black luxury car to visit the Take Wing Center. The main road from Maison Chance to Take Wing Center was being built so we had to use the old dirt road on the side.

The rainy season was still with us, so the road was bumpy and muddy. I joked that in Vietnam pot holes were normally call "chicken holes", but now they were called "elephant holes" to describe the condition of the road!

We drove past the land I was buying for the Village Chance project, now it was just a large water pond with people busy harvesting the water spinach that was growing wild and catching small, sweet field crabs. Our beautiful car drove slowly behind a team of motorcyclists leading the way for the Foreign Affairs motorcade. The riders looked hassled and struggled with the pot holes and the puddles, some of them over 60-feet long. Every now and then I had to put my head out of the window to give them encouragement. This official visit was originally planned for 30 minutes, but finally it was prolonged to over two and a half hours. Mrs. Leuthardt was seriously interested in the works of Maison Chance. After the visit she gave me big hug saying, "We will help you."

We had just started this new project and we needed a lot of help in every phase. I sought free advice from a number of architects abroad over the design of Village Chance.

The first plan was quite simple and practical, with a single floor and thatched roof. I thought it would be quite picturesque, but I changed my idea after thinking over the extra cost of keeping thatched roof free of insects.

## *Cindy Livingston*

At that fateful point, a famous businesswoman found out about the work being done by Maison Chance. An American, she was the CEO of the watch company GUESS, but her company was based in Switzerland. She had over 60 retail shops all over the world. The company celebrated its twenty-year anniversary in 2007 and to mark the occasion, Cindy Livingston decided to support some charity organisations in third world countries.

After reading our report on the Project Village Chance, Mrs. Livingston came to Vietnam to directly learn more about Maison Chance. She arrived late at night, so I picked her up early the next morning.

We came on our Whale Bus to pick her up her hotel which was right next to the Opera House.

She was quite brown with long silver hair and very polite. The bus had no air conditioning; therefore, it was extremely hot and humid. But we launched our conversation straight into the Village Chance project. Then I took her to visit the other establishments of Maison Chance. The tour took a bit of time, but she looked pleased and showed her interest.

By the afternoon, I was still thinking when she took the lead and said: "What do you think of a million US dollars donation to Maison Chance from me?" I could not believe my ears. I replied, "This is a big amount of money; I cannot imagine what it looks like. But to get that donation, what do I have to do? A 100-page document?" She only laughed and said, "No, no, just three pages would be enough!"

*"I made long journeys to different parts of the world to share the lives of less fortunate individuals with all my heart. And yet now, at this moment, I had to squeeze my brain to defend myself against attacks from my enemies, and I did not even know their identities.*
*The two events happened as planned but in a much more somber atmosphere."*

# CHAPTER 14

# *A Stormy Year*

In early February 2008, a few days before the year of the Mouse (Mau Ty) began, someone warned me, "This year will be your 'age year', the Year of the Mouse. Take care."

## *My Accident*

That year Trung decided to come to Vietnam to celebrate *Tết*, the Vietnamese New Year, with us. He would stay at Maison Chance until the end of February. This year was a leap year so there were 29 days in February; but this was not any ordinary February.

A few days before Trung returned to the US, Miss Ky Duyen, the Master of Ceremonies of "Paris By Night" happened to be in Saigon and she invited me to her home for dinner to introduce me to possible future sponsors for Maison Chance.

I was extremely busy at that time preparing for my trip to Canada and America in March and her house was very far from us. I did not want to go but Ky Duyen would not accept my refusal so finally I had to go. I took Trung on my motorbike with me as my passenger, and on the way home we had a serious accident.

When I woke up, I found myself in a hospital bed. Trung, covered in blood, was on the stretcher next to me. All I felt was the pain all over my body. I did not remember seeing the accident happen, so I could not answer any questions which the police fired at me. Trung and I could not remember what happen exactly.

According to the police, the accident occurred at the corner of two streets. The motorcyclist who hit us head on did not wear a safety helmet and he died instantly. Hearing this news, I felt an emotional pain even sharper than the one I was experiencing in my body now. I found out that I had a broken arm, an injured leg, and my lungs did not feel great.

About eight in the morning next day we were transferred to the Orthopaedic Trauma Center where I knew quite a few of the doctors in the spinal ward since they cared for some patients from Maison Chance.

I struggled to breath and coughed up blood, so I was put on an oxygen tank.

Slowly the memory of the accident returned to me, but one thing was gone and could not be retrieved; the dead motorcyclist was still at the morgue. He was only 28. His mother was devastated by his death and could not be comforted by any means. I wanted to attend his funeral, but I was too weak to move. A week later I asked for leave from the hospital, so I could attend the ceremony of the opening of his grave for his soul to be released permanently.

This is a custom of the Buddhists from the South. They believe the soul of the deceased needed to be released from the sealed grave after he was interred for three days; thus, the grave opening ceremony.

Speechless, I held his mother in my arms. Then I followed his family to the pagoda to pray for his released soul.

Trung recovered well and he returned to California. I had to stay put to recover from my injuries. The trip to North America had to be postponed.

Three months after the accident, I still had a pain in my head. My doctor sent me to be X-rayed and tested. They found that there was a small crack on my skull, so they prescribed a special medication loaded with calcium and the crack slowly healed. All I had left was a hollow indentation on my temple.

I was lucky that I wore a safety helmet and had a hard head naturally!

At Tết (New Year), I was warned about "my age" year and that it would be an eventful year, but I only laughed. I am not a superstitious person and life is not all white or all black; life follows the basic principle of positive versus negative. A lot of Asians believe in this; that is, in the good there was the bad and also the reverse. While in recovery, I received hundreds of communications supporting me and Maison Chance. The accident was bad luck but then there were other instances of good fortune.

I had to cancel my trip to North America but, because of the accident, the push for establishing Maison Chance elsewhere became more urgent. Maison Chance US and Maison Chance Canada were being formed and my Australian friends were also interested in inviting me to visit Australia when I was well again.

## *The Construction of Village Chance*

Nothing happens without a cause. Since I postponed my trip, I had more time to look at my Village Chance project.

For over a year now, there were several distinct plans for Village Chance proposed by different volunteer architects. I asked my friend Mrs. Trang, the lady whose company built the Take Wing Center, to help me design a plan with all the features offered in the architects' existing plans. I also asked her to participate in my new project as well and she accepted.

The present plan showed a structure of five different blocks joined together with small bridges, ramps, corridor passages and elevators. Each block was dedicated to different usages and functions. The first three blocks were to contain 40 apartments, each suitable for a family with at least one disabled person. Another block was designated to be the new school. It would replace the school classrooms in the Take Wing Center where a space for product manufacturing was desperately needed.

The fifth block would have three floors facing the street, where I proposed to open a restaurant operated by the residents of Maison Chance. They would be trained in cookery and restaurant management.

One reason for this was that the children would have a skill in their hands and the restaurant would be a perfect place for Maison Chance's residents to interact with the local community. The restaurant would occupy two floors with the extra floor serving as a canteen for the school kids.

We also planned to have a central courtyard in the middle of the five blocks so that at break time the kids could play in the yard safely and the disabled people in wheelchairs could play sports and exercise.

I also thought of a therapeutic swimming pool for physiotherapy treatment where the disabled and the children could learn to swim.

Also, in my mind were a few guest rooms for normal and disabled guests alike.

\*\*\*

After the YouTube clip on Maison Chance, my DVD was released in December 2007. Then the news of my accident was posted and went viral. Maison Chance and its founder became the topic of conversation among the Vietnamese overseas. Tim was not the first person who did charity work here, but what intrigued them was that I was a foreigner, I was not a nun, and I could speak Vietnamese fluently.

## The First Time in Australia

In September 2008 I was invited to visit Australia by the Vietnam Foundation of Australia.

I brought 20 paintings with me to be auctioned off at the fund-raising functions in Sydney, Canberra, Brisbane and Melbourne.

The Vietnam Foundation organized the first function for me at a large Chinese restaurant. The dining room was huge and overcrowded; nine hundred guests came to find out more about Maison Chance. Almost all of the attendees were of Vietnamese origin. To show my respect and gratitude to my sponsor I wore a Vietnamese dress. This was the third time I appeared in a traditional Vietnamese dress.

I talked about Maison Chance and showed some documentaries on the current Vietnam.

I was very surprised at the number of people who wanted to meet me, to hold my hand, to be photographed with me and to hand me their envelopes or to have me sign the painting which they just bought.

They all seem to know me, but as for me I did not even know where I was standing.

This was September, and Tim did not realize that it was winter in the land of the kangaroos! This is where I was taught a new Vietnamese phrase: "Danh bo cap." It means shivering with the cold and the teeth chattering. I had not needed this expression for the last 15 years in Vietnam.

The next morning, I visited the nuns and the Buddhist worshippers at the Phap Bao Pagoda. We left for Canberra immediately after our vegetarian lunch. Canberra was a small capital city for a large continental country. We drove past the gum tree forests and every now and then some kangaroos on the side of the road stared at the passing car. Inevitably, a few animals got run over by trucks at night, but this could happen anywhere. All through the trip I had my eyes glued on the window trying to catch a glimpse of koalas hanging on tree branches.

After my presentation in Canberra, we went to Brisbane where two functions were organized for me.

The first fund raising was a banquet dinner at a private home. It was prepared, cooked and presented by Lien Yeomans. She was a small lady but her talent for cooking was large. She arrived in Australia when she was sixteen and had been living here for over 40 years. Her house was very beautiful. There were only 12 guests and each donated 500 Australian dollars to help Maison Chance and to taste an exquisite banquet.

Lien was also an artist and she designed and decorated her home and looked after a large garden full of exotic flora and fauna. I saw strange giant rats hanging around on her trees but the 'rats' turned out to be Australian possums, a kind of giant marsupial with a bushy tail.

I talked to Lien about my plan for the restaurant at Village Chance. She promised she would come to help organize the kitchen and train the children in cooking and kitchen maintenance, and she kept her promise.

The next day, the Phat Da Pagoda held a big meeting that was very friendly and simple. Over 600 people turned up for my talk and to support Maison Chance.

My next stop was Melbourne, where there were also two big events organized for me. I was met at the airport and taken straight to the Quang Minh Pagoda. When we were about a little over half a mile from the pagoda, the driver pointed out to me, "Look, the road is parked out for the first time. They've all come to listen to you."

As soon as I walked into the pagoda I realized that over a thousand people came to hear me.

The meeting was simple and easy, and we had tea and biscuits for refreshments. The audience's enthusiasm and their generous support really moved me to tears. Even the tears of a hard head like me could not restraint themselves and they rolled down my face.

That afternoon, Miss Ngoc Lan, who planned the program, and her friends hosted another event for me at a restaurant. At first, they booked one whole floor for 450 people, but the tickets sold out quickly, so they booked another floor for another 350 guests. That night both Lan and I took turns running up and down between the two floors to meet and greet our supporters. The band helped out when we need a rest. The auction sale of the painting was very successful, and all 16 paintings were sold. One of them brought in over 3,000 Australian dollars. I was surprised and grateful at the generous support and I was so happy to see that so many disregarded the distance they traveled to come to help the less fortunate.

## *In North America*

That October I went to North America to attend meetings organized by the Maison Chance Association Canada and in the US. They were both founded recently. I arrived at Toronto first, then Ottawa and Montreal. People had learned about me and Maison Chance though the media and I was greeted in Canada as warmly as when I was in Australia. I was treated as if I was an old relative.

I left Canada to go to the United States with Thu Hien, a little orphan girl from Maison Chance. She came along to tell her own story and to describe Maison Chance. We stopped at nine destinations including Washington, D.C., Philadelphia, Houston and Texas. Miss Ky Duyen volunteered to be our MC for the meetings with the local supporters.

The biggest meeting was in Houston which 1,100 people attended. Before going onto the stage Hien said to me, "It is so cold in here that maybe the air conditioner is on the coolest setting." I borrowed a jacket for Hien from a woman nearby. It was too large, but it helped to keep Hien warm. Miss Ky Duyen noticed that Hien was shivering in her chair, so she inquired if Hien was anxious about appearing in front of the crowd. Hien laughed and replied. "I'm shivering because I am cold, not because I am afraid." It was true that when Hien first arrived she was a bit timid about being interviewed by the newspapers, but after a week she was now a perfect ambassador for Maison Chance.

*The dinner in Vancouver in October of 2008.*

We caught up with Trung in Los Angeles. He had come on an eight-hour bus trip from Sacramento. He acted as our public relation officer, as our driver and he took on any other jobs that needed to be done. He moved baggage from here to there, made arrangements for all the events and was in charge of all bookkeeping responsibilities, including recording the proceeds from all fund-raising events.

Seattle, a city on the coast of Pacific Ocean near the border with Canada, was the last stop before we finished the US tour. After the function at the Tea Palace restaurant, I said goodbye to Hien. She did not have a visa for Canada, so I continued on my way to Vancouver and Calgary without her.

Seattle is 168 miles from Vancouver and my friends from Canada decided to drive back there with me that night. They had come down to Seattle to hear my talk and we had to bring the auctioned paintings to Canada. We hid them on the floor of the car in case we ran into a problem with the border police, so we were a bit scared as they checked our passports and let us go.

We arrived at Vancouver at 6 a.m. and that afternoon I had to present my Maison Chance project at a function.

In Vancouver the atmosphere of the function was quite difference from the subdued atmosphere in Seattle.

The room could hold 580 guests but by the end they managed to fit another 200. It was so noisy that guests had to shout to hear one another; but in an atmosphere of social equality and simplicity. They all looked happy and the tables were full of food and drinks. There were no gaps between people; if Hien were here she would not have been able to move her wheelchair between the rows of chairs.

I was wondering if they would stop talking to listen to me. But soon after I started my talk the room was completely silent. I did not even have to ask permission to speak as I did at some other functions where the audience was a bit older.

During the evening I often heard people comment that most of the Vietnamese in Vancouver had turned up for this function. Usually the Vancouver Vietnamese divided themselves into smaller groups depending on their politics, religion or social class. Tonight, they all gathered together with an open heart and mind to learn about the lives of the less fortunate in Vietnam.

The next day we flew to Calgary with three members of Maison Chance Canada. Calgary is an oil rich city which has attracted many Vietnamese who came to build a better life, at least financially.

Calgary is up in the mountains and it was November and bitterly cold. The landscape looked a bit sad.

The meeting that afternoon was much more sombre than normal, and the audience appeared to be of a better class. However, there was no food, only light refreshments. The atmosphere was quite stiff, and everyone listened in silence.

At question time, a man of about 60 stood up and started talking: 'We are the boat people who escaped from Vietnam after 1975. We admire your work helping the poor in Vietnam and we want to support you, but if we gave you some money would you have to give it to the government and can the government control your bank account?'

I explained to him clearly that our organisation has NGO status and we have permission to operate as a charity. I explained that I am the bank account holder and no one else can control my account. And since I founded Maison Chance, all the cash we spent was properly recorded.

## A Matter of Politics

That was not the first time I was queried about this matter. During my trip to Northern America, I was always cautioned about being transparent about my work in Vietnam, the country which these people had to leave behind 30 years ago.

Four days after I came back to Vietnam, there was a big discussion on the internet. Some posts attacked me, accusing me of "being a spy for the communist government of Vietnam" or "refusing to pay respect to the old Vietnamese flag of yellow with three red lines but worshipping the new red flag with the yellow star!" This latter accusation had a photograph attached.

These people were extremely anti-communist. They had searched the Internet and found a photo taken in 2002 when I received the Henry Dunant award. The photo showed me, the orphans and the disabled on the stage singing a song about Maison Chance. Behind us were the flags of Vietnam and the flag of Switzerland. (See the photo on page 90.) The flags were in the background only because I had requested that I receive the award in Vietnam and in the presence of representatives from both Switzerland and Vietnam. I had hoped that by doing this I could prove to the Vietnamese authorities that Switzerland officially recognized Maison Chance as a legitimate organisation and that fact would help us to be recognized by the local authority as well.

## My Trip to Europe and the Warning

After being home only for six days, I had to fly to Europe. This time I would go to London first since a musician friend had organized an event with 500 Vietnamese. My friend was courageous because he went ahead with the program in spite of many anonymous warnings that if he held the meetings he would meet with unfortunate incidents. But a lot of people traveled a long way to London to attend my talk on Maison Chance, so he remained calm and carried out the plan.

When I arrived, no guest came forward to shake hands with me as normal. Afterwards I discovered that these were Vietnamese from the North who had migrated to Great Britain for economic reasons. The atmosphere warmed up after a cool start and the art auction was enthusiastically successful. I was wrong to think that in Europe it would be different; the meeting turned out to be a success.

From there I went to France, where Maison Chance France had organized a special meeting in Paris for me. The organizers had also received threats, but the meeting was still held. On the night of the event, there were four elderly men at the entrance holding up placards and handing out leaflets saying "Mat Goc" (meaning Lost Roots). Their message was "Do not support this event; it has been organized by the communists". However, a lot of people turned up and the demonstrators left at the request of the police.

Then I continued to Switzerland to attend the annual meeting of Maison Chance Swiss. The guests were half Swiss and half Vietnamese and at question time I asked if the audience knew about the flag story. They all nodded and laughed. However, I wanted to make my position clear to all my supporters that we were a non-political organisation and our activities were in the social services.

I continued my explanation to find out if they had more questions but they all shook their head and laughed as well.

With the Vietnamese living in Switzerland I did not have to explain too much, they understood my situation.

However, I ran into difficulties on my trip to Germany. When our volunteers from Munich began to organize a meeting for me, they were also threatened anonymously. This time the volunteers decided to cancel the event since they were quite scared that their houses would be burnt down. The situation was tense. On top of that I was continuously attacked on the Internet for reasons I did not understand. However, I tried to remain calm, to defend myself and to react positively to any hostility. I myself received anonymous telephone calls threatening me that if I were to go to Germany I would be met with unfortunate accidents.

Besides Munich, our plan for Germany was also to attend meetings in Frankfurt and Cologne. Now I asked myself if was wise to abandon these two meetings? From Switzerland, I telephoned the organizers for those two events to find out if they wished to keep the meetings. They wanted to meet me. They were not scared by the threats and they believed that if I canceled the meetings the extremist would have the reason to believe that I was under the control of the communists. I made a long trip to come here to tell my supporters with all my heart about the lives of the less fortunate and yet I had to think hard about how to defend myself against the attacks of my unknown enemies. We held the two meetings but in a much more restrained atmosphere.

................................................

After four months of travelling non-stop by different modes of transportation, I got home at the end of the year, fatigued but happy.

My father, Laurent decided to come to celebrate the New Year in Vietnam with us. He had never been to Vietnam. In 2001 he helped us with 20 computers as a member of Maison Chance Swiss. He was a journalist, so he also helped us publish a quarterly newsletter.

On December 31, he welcomed in New Year's Eve with the children and the disabled residents in the front courtyard of Maison Chance. He was much moved and they all called him grandfather. He sang a lot of spiritual and gospels songs for us, the special music of the former black slaves of North America. I explained to my children that in the last few years my father had organized many musical events to raise funds for us and this gave some ideas to the musicians at Maison Chance.

*"When the Village Chance, the 'Lucky Village' was opened on January 20, 2011 over 700 people came to celebrate. Children, the disabled residents, staff members of Maison Chance, other organisations, friends and supporters from all over the world all gathered here."*

# CHAPTER 15

# *Village Chance,*
# *The Lucky Village*

The year of the Buffalo, 2009, was arriving. For over a year now new chapters of the international association of Maison Chance were appearing everywhere. I was the sole person to communicate any news of Maison Chance Vietnam. But I thought perhaps to keep the financial matters transparent I should reorganize the management team so that they could administer the whole organisation. I also asked myself what images and values I wished to project for Maison Chance.

Right at the beginning, Maison Chance Vietnam declared its non-political status. However, after the flag incident I had to put a strong emphasis on the neutral nature of the Maison Chance activities.

We are definitely humanitarian and non-political.

## *The Birth of International Association for Maison Chance*

On April 26, 2009, a meeting of volunteers from six different countries was held in Lyon. As a result, Foundation Maison Chance

International was born as an instrument to coordinate all planned international activities operated under the banner of Maison Chance Vietnam. A major goal of the new Foundation was to ensure the transparency of the operating costs of its activities.

## The Lost Children

On June 25, 2009 I was in my bedroom playing with my children when I heard the news of the death of the singer Michael Jackson. I was devastated and sad as I read all the news available on his death. I admired and respected him. He was a very special person; a genius with a giant heart. His passion for music inspired so many people and moved so many hearts.

On August 22 of the same year of 2009, more sad news hit me. My dear friend Trung, the secretary of Maison Chance USA, was killed in a traffic accident. It happened late at night at an intersection where a truck hit his car head on and he died instantly. I could not believe my ears; my tears ran down my face. I had never felt so sad at the death of a person as I did for Trung. A year and a half previously Trung and I had escaped death, and we prayed and thanked God for having spared our lives. But this time, at 45, Trung left us permanently. And how important this brother Trung was for me! His wise words and his presence helped me to overcome so many challenges.

Like all other supporters, Trung worked tirelessly to make the Village Chance Project became a reality. People like Trung helped us to start this pioneering project which gave the less fortunate a new and better life.

## The Laying of the Foundation Stone

On the morning of October 27, 2009, the foundation stone was laid to start the construction of Village Chance, or 'The Lucky

Village'. All members of Maison Chance, the staff of the Nam Thien Loc construction company and other persons associated with the project were present for this occasion. We stood on the land next to it because our block of land was still under water. It had to be filled in and raised up another five feet.

The project would take 14 months to complete, but my friend Mrs. Trang understood that many families were waiting for an apartment in this building complex, so she would use all her power to have it built in the shortest time possible.

By early 2010, the year of the Tiger, my block of swampy terrain was transformed into high and dry land and a brick fence surrounding the block had just been constructed. Now our 4,100 square yards of land stood out among the neighboring blocks. Then the first building was built. This was a big project and I needed to watch it daily to guarantee a good result.

At the same time, we had the Maison Chance renovated. The local authorities asked for the return of the land which we had been given permission to use 15 years earlier. It was right next to the first home we had bought, and it measured 107 square yards. But now in order to accommodate everyone we had to remodel the facility. This was also an opportunity to raise the floor up a meter so that it was not lower than the road; before it had always flooded whenever it rained. This renovation took five months to complete and we had to move to the Take Wing Center temporarily during which the production rooms, the classrooms, and the corridors overflowed with people.

This was when I went to India for a month.

## The Trip to India

I was curious to know how India dealt with the most disadvantaged population and I knew all the places I wanted to visit.

I also knew I needed to quickly organize this trip; if it got postponed I would not have another opportunity.

Tim had an affiliation with India since 2005 when we were still building the Take Wing Center. At that time, I received a big fat envelope from India with pictures of Krabi children, a minority group in the Northeast India in the state of Assam. The sender of this envelope was Uttam Teron and he was determined to help wipe out literacy in this poorest region in India. He learned about the existence of Maison Chance though a magazine and he wished to share his experiences in developing action programs for humanity assistance with me.

We had been in contact by correspondence for a few years and I promised I would arrange my time to visit him.

Before going to India, I had made contact with people who were responsible for charitable projects in different regions, especially those of Terre des Hommes, Alsace, one of the participating partners of Maison Chance for a few years. Before launching into the Maison Chance undertaking, I did some research on other projects which cared for the disabled and orphans in Europe, but soon I realized their methods were not suitable for the environment of Vietnam. Therefore, I switched my interests to those organizations working in third world countries under similar conditions and I tried to observe their methodology.

In May 2010 I flew to Calcutta; the city of Mother Theresa and the untouchables, the bottom class of society. I stayed in India for a month to observe the projects which were similar to mine.

The visits to these places were very interesting but also required hard work. I witnessed so many difficulties, both materially and physically in this country.

Everywhere the houses had fallen down in a tattered state and yet people were still waiting for the gods to fix them up. The majority of the population are Hindu, so they are vegetarians and they believe in reincarnation. Also, their relationship with nature and others differed a great deal from that of the West. They remained a mystery to the Westerners.

Every day I shared their food with them; the same meal of bread, potatoes and rice with curry sauce.

Hundreds of sick and homeless people lived on the streets; dirty streets full of pot holes and rubbish everywhere. Dogs, monkeys, cows and goats lived among the people.

I often saw dead people and animals on the side of the road. The luckier corpses were thrown into the sacred river by the untouchables, the lowest class in society who were only fit for the dirtiest jobs. I got to know some of them. They were born untouchables, so they lived in the utmost poverty and they accepted the fate into which they were born.

I also noticed that any humanitarian project in India had to face two obstacles: the belief in a human's pre-destined fate and the social class system. There was hardly any concept of mutual assistance.

I felt the need to meet the social reformists who were fighting for human rights for the untouchables; some of these were very experienced but other like Uttam still had a long way to go.

Based on my own experience, I had a few wise words for them. In turn, I received advice from my new friends on internal administration, the reception of volunteers and the how to manage the beneficiaries return to society.

On this trip, I had met people who shared my own ideals, people who sacrificed the body and soul of their own personal life to help those less fortunate than us. We shared our work experiences, our challenges and our hopes. This was a rare occasion for all of us and it encouraged us and helped us to enrich our minds for future projects.

This trip also taught me that I could not help every single less fortunate person; I could only assist those who really wanted to change their own fate. I also felt that Vietnam would have enough resources to help their poor people to have better life and that Vietnam recognized that my works in my adopted country were useful and meaningful.

........................................................

By the end of 2010, the construction site of Village Chance was overcrowded; when all the trades were required to work at once there could be more than 300 workers on site, all doing their bits for the project. By then, all five blocks of buildings were constructed and only the completion of the main gate, some painting and renovations and interior decoration remained.

We planted four large trees next to the main gate and three flame trees (Poinciana) in the courtyard. I also added two milkwood pines (Alstonia) for their fragrant flowers. A fence of small bamboo completed the landscaping.

## New Accommodation for Family with Disabled Members

Village Chance or the "Lucky Village" was officially opened on January 20, 2011. More than 700 guests attended including the children and the disabled, staff members of Maison Chance and all associated partners as well as friends and supporters from all over the world.

This third establishment was very beautiful, and I was in debt to all my sponsors who had contributed into this project from day one until now.

The day after the opening, Village Chance welcomed its first residents; Thu Hien, Lanh and their daughters were the first to move in just a few days before the New Year of the Cat (Tan. Mao) in February (according to the sun calendar). Hien's new apartment had three windows and three separate rooms, quite unlike their old rented place. The apartment was designed for wheelchair access, so Hien could move about with ease. The walls were painted blue, like the color of a bright beautiful day. They did not miss their old place which had flooded every time it rained and was not at all suitable for someone in a wheelchair.

*Tim at the opening of Village Chance.*

*A basketball game in the courtyard.*

The other families followed Hien to move into the Village and within six months half of the total numbers of apartments in the Village were occupied by families with one or more disabled members in wheelchairs.

Right from the beginning, the mutually supporting life style shared by the disabled and the healthy at Maison Chance was now being repeated at Village Chance. The orphans from Maison Chance came over to visit the disabled and to entertain their small children. In the afternoon there was usually a basketball game in the courtyard between the wheelchair riders. Some were not even disabled but they had to sit in the chairs to play.

Everywhere at any time of the day there were crowds of people of all kinds and of all ages sitting together socialising.

Soon, after years of growing up and being educated at Maison Chance, many of our beneficiaries began to fly out of the nest equipped with a new pair of wings. Some went back to the country; some had to stay on at the Village because of their disability. The majority of them were married with children so I had been promoted to the title of paternal grandmother (ba noi) as well as maternal grandmother (ba ngoai).

Some who were childless due to their handicap were happy to adopt.

As this is written, I am only over 40 years old and yet I have more than 60 grandchildren. Some live at Village Chance, others live elsewhere.

It was a challenge for parents with handicapped children to find a place for them in childcare centers since children with any disability were not generally accepted and other kids had to be over two years of age. Moreover, the childcare fee was far too high compared to their parent's income.

I also realized that physically handicapped children could not get to the childcare centers by themselves and those centers were not really equipped with suitable facilities anyway. We had to find the answer for this problem ourselves, so we opened a childcare center in the Village. Our fee was less than half of traditional centers and we accepted children with handicaps and at six months old.

*Song, a resident without limbs who swam like a fish in the swimming pool at Village Chance.*

## *Maria Saegesser*

I had the idea about building apartments suitable for the handicapped, but I had no appreciation of the technical design details. Luckily a lady who assisted us in the planning was an expert in designing for the handicapped. She was Maria Saegesser, founder of the charitable organisation "Atelier Amitie" (or Friendship Workshop) and ambassador for the Masikini Foundation, who had helped us so many times, especially in the purchase of the land. In 2007, when I was in Switzerland, I telephoned her for the first time. We met at a restaurant at Lausanne Station. We got on very well and from then on whenever we met it would be at a station somewhere such as Bale, Zurich, Bern, or Vevey.

Maria came into my life like a Fairy Godmother in an old fairy tale. I did not have to ask, and she knew all our needs and provided us with the solutions. Now, with the support of the Masikini Foundation we could help the poorest to have a better life.

In one of these meeting, Maria gave me a bottle containing 32 corn seeds and wondered if I could guess their meaning. I looked puzzled and was unable to guess, so she explained to me that each seed represented 10,000 Swiss Francs. I was completely surprised that 320,000 Swiss Francs was the equivalent of 340,000 US dollars, a sum which was exactly what I needed to renovate the village. Our prayers had been answered. We now could also afford the magic comfort for our less fortunate people.

One of the infrastructure features we wanted to include in the project was a therapeutic swimming pool.

Swimming would help the disabled to relax and relieve their pain. We planned for a heated therapeutic pool with warm water above 86 degrees Fahrenheit to help the patients unwind and help keeping their bodies flexible. The other function of the pool was to teach children of Maison Chance how to swim.

In Vietnam there were many drowning incidents, so our planned swimming pool would suit both functions and one day my orphaned children would be swimming like fish in water.

## The Restaurant at Village Chance

We planned to open a restaurant at Village Chance operated by healthy disadvantaged persons.

My friend Lien, the talented cook from Australia, kept her promise to come and help us set up the kitchen and to train a dozen youths to cook and to manage the restaurant to an international standard. She came first to help remodel and upgrade the kitchen and some months later she returned to run a training course. Her experience helped us to understand the food industry; however, our address was not convenient for our desired clientele.

## The Adventure with Croissant

Croissants are delicious. However, there was only a kind of croissant in Vietnam; it is called the "buffalo horn" cake. But as for a real croissant, the kind that was crispy outside but soft and velvety inside, I had not seen one here yet.

I had survived on rice for the last twenty years; if I did not like rice I probably would have left Vietnam a long time ago. I did not miss Western food much, except every now and then I wished for a real croissant. I tried to have them whenever I was in Europe.

Twenty years ago, on my way to Vietnam, I rode across the grasslands of Mongolia and learned that their daily meal was plain boiled mutton without any other condiments. They also milked their horses and kept the milk in a large vat left in the middle of their tent. There was always some yellow fatty cream floating on the surface, so the Mongolians manufactured cheese from horse milk as well. These were lumps of hardened milk as solid as stone and very sour. This cheese was stored on the roof of their tent. I remember clearly every morning when I woke up that I had had a dreamed of croissants.

Twenty years later, the croissant still in my dream. In Vietnam, only some five stars hotels had them on the menu. I thought, maybe this could be a good business for us.

A Belgian supporter of Maison Chance, who had discovered Maison Chance through different sources and my talks in Belgium, was visiting us at that time. He sponsored a class to teach patisserie to the less fortunate there. He kindly introduced to me one of the graduates who studied patisserie for the last six years and who now worked at an international hotel in Saigon's business center. Happily, he accepted our request and came to teach our patisserie students at Village Chance. And so, the adventure of the croissant began.

*The croissant*

# *Father Christmas*

Christmas was usually celebrated at Maison Chance but in 2012 for the first time our Christmas was held at Village Chance.

Like every other year, Thành was Father Christmas; it had become a tradition in our family. Thành, with his bushy white beard and red clothes, was good in this role. But he felt really itchy and sweaty under his heavy costume so he only lasted 15 minutes in it. I reminded Thành that he had to behave like a proper Father Christmas, so he put on the costume again. He was very proud of his annual role. So, whenever visitors came he asked them if they knew that he was Father Christmas!

Thành started the festivities with his ritual, holding the microphone and wishing everyone a good Christmas. Thành was in his element; normally he could not utter many words. With passion he told the 250 guests present that December 24 is the birthday of Jesus Christ, that he brought happiness to many people and he was an example for all of us because he had sacrificed his life for the less fortunate. Thành said in his own words,

"Jesus Christ accepted and helped the most unfortunate people, like Thành who was the first member of Maison Chance where we learned to love one another and help one another."

Then Thành took the candies out of his bag and offered them to the children before he had to go to the grotto where 250 presents were waiting to be distributed.

The last song for the party was in the lively, energetic Gangnam Style and the rhythm of this song encouraged people to dance. Everybody was on the dance floor; from the young to the elderly and from the healthy to the disabled in their wheelchairs. It was truly an experience of a moment of innocent enjoyment in a sharing atmosphere.

*Tim with Thành, Father Christmas (©McFreddy Photos)*

*"After 20 years, I truly understood the saying: 'A drop of water in the ocean, a grain of sand in the desert' or, more correctly, 'a grain of rice in the bowl of the starving people'."*

# CHAPTER 16

# Twenty Years Went by as Fast as a Monsoon Downpour

I had been witnessing the super-fast developments in Vietnam. Early 1993, I was in Hue, the old capital of the former emperors of the Nguyen Dynasty. On the banks of the Huong River there were small bookshops selling newly published books on studying the English language which were very popular among the students.

In Saigon, most people rode bicycles and only the wealthy could afford motorcycles. There were hardly any cars, only a few hundred small taxis painted white with blue stripes and used mainly to take passengers from the airport to the city center. There was no public transport then, only a few traffic lights and motorcyclists did not wear safety helmets. There were hardly any high-rise buildings except a few international hotels in the city center. There was no fashion at all! The peasants dressed traditionally, and the city people dressed mostly in the uniforms of their work places.

There were only three television channels and the broadcasting stopped at 10 p.m. Some magazines started to appear but not as many as now. Telephones were rare, but a fax machine was even more difficult to find. Photocopying was not yet popular. In addition, there were many beggars, homeless people and street kids. The most pitiful were the young children, the disabled and the homeless elderly.

However, changes were fast and furious as high-rise buildings mushroomed up everywhere. Machine-made goods replaced hand-made products and the streets were tarred over and equipped with sidewalks. And thatched roofs were replaced by tin roofs.

Then fashion, magazines and music, especially foreign music, exploded in the open market.

Only a few years of changes and Saigon was transformed completely; it became more open and more modern.

Since I had arrived here, this country had changed enormously. However, social services had not kept pace and up to that time the authorities still did not have any solutions for the most unfortunate class, which was under our care.

When I thought of all this, I felt satisfied with my own work. The members of Maison Chance had escaped their miserable fate and found themselves a place under the sun. They have now moved on. They have their own homes and are living independently with their families. Their places in Maison Chance are taken up by the new less fortunate children.

Vietnam is constantly changed economically, but the services offered to the poor, the unfortunate and the disabled are still lacking.

Maison Chance is the only place to care for the seriously paralyzed residents. We offer them long-term care and training. We have also established suitable education and vocational training for the unfortunate street kids and orphans. We created a cozy family for all our beneficiaries, so they could flourish.

Since living with us, these people have changed into new individuals living healthy lives according to the philosophy of Maison Chance. They are the people who understand our ideal the most.

Today Maison Chance employs 20 former members, among them a few university graduates. One of them, a graduate in Education and Teaching, has replaced Teacher Tung to look after the educational system. Another graduated in management in the US and she is now back in Vietnam to assist me in the running of Maison Chance. An illiterate quadriplegic who came to Maison Chance at 13 went to school with us and later learned to speak French. Now he is in charge of our website and he receives all French speaking visitors at Maison Chance.

The children of Maison Chance are our future. They will be the leaders of tomorrow.

## The Twentieth Anniversary Celebration at the Saigon Opera House

I chose the Saigon Grand Opera House as the location to celebrate the twentieth anniversary of Maison Chance but that year there was only ONE remaining date available for us: Friday, July 5, 2013.

When the big day arrived, 350 guests including children, adults, the disabled and the staff of Maison Chance were in turn transported in our new bus. The vehicle was modified to be able to easily load the wheelchairs and for people to get in and out without needing assistance. Our driver made many trips to transport our people and the goods required for the event to the Opera House by the afternoon.

The Grand Opera House in Saigon was built by the French in 1900 and there are no access provisions for the handicapped and there is no loading zone. There is only the magnificent and opulent front

*Our new bus taking us to the Opera House on our big day, July 5, 2013.*

entrance with many steps, so we had to construct three ramps for our wheelchair riders.

I chose the opera house deliberately to celebrate this important occasion, but I overlooked the fact that we had to use a large professional stage. And we were not professional performers.

So, I began the introduction to this special occasion by saying that this was the first time that we had appeared in front of the general public and that we wished to share the results of what we had achieved in the last twenty years. To do this we would share the stories of the twenty families who outgrew Maison Chance to be independent individuals with cozy families, children and a skill in their hands. These people symbolized the work of Maison Chance.

We began with a 30 second film clip showing the daily life of the first family at Maison Chance. As the clip faded out, the light shone brightly on the main characters standing on the stage.

A smiling lady in a wheelchair with her husband and two children at her side slowly moved toward the front of the stage to greet the audience and to introduce herself and her family to them. In turn twenty families followed one another to appear in the spot light and to tell the audience the story of their lives.

The audience was very enthusiastic about the next film clip introducing Han and Ngoc. Han not only had no use of one of his arms and both of his legs, but he could hardly speak. And yet he himself spoke the introduction in the clip. Then out of darkness under the bright spot light Han and his family appeared. Both Han and Ngoc were in wheelchairs, holding each other's hand they slowly rolled to the front. She was waiting to give birth to her baby and we got her out of the hospital for the special event.

After the family presentation, an exotic dance was performed by ten wheelchair riders. Ten quadriplegics "danced" their wheelchairs to very loud and fast music. They turned right, then left, then this way and that way. They waved proudly to the audience with their withered arms. They were the real stars of tonight.

The last item on the program was the auction of three paintings by disabled artists. Each artist took turns introducing their works to the audience and stated that all the proceeds from the auction would be donated to the new project of Maison Chance. Even though their mobility was limited they felt very proud that they could help others who were less fortunate than they are.

As Vuong, the last painter, rolled his wheelchair onto the stage he looked a bit pale and shaky. I knew that he was in pain and could not speak, so I took the microphone from him and explained that Vuong was not well. "His spinal cord is not straight it prevents him breathing properly and it also causes him a lot of pain so Vuong had to use his elbows to support himself in the chairs." I explained that Vuong was only twenty-one, but he had to be operated on or he would die. I described how we had been searching for a specialist who could

*Dancing in electric wheelchairs at the Saigon Opera House, at the 20th anniversary of Maison Chance.*

perform this task and finally we found an expert in France, but we didn't have enough money to pay for the operation yet.

From the audience, one guest raised his hand saying: "Please allow me to pay for Vuong's air ticket to express my admiration of your courage." Another person offered to pay for the cost of Vuong's care.

To conclude the evening, all of us Maison Chance people appeared on stage to say good bye and to thank our guests for their support by a special song: "The Maison Chance Song."

At 3:30 in the morning the blue bus picked up the last lot of passengers who waited patiently in high spirits at the steps of the Opera House. In the bus someone suggested some dancing music and this dance continued on the bus until the morning.

## The Following New Ideas

After 20 years we are still on track and following the original ideal to help every member of Maison Chance to have an independent life and to be able to re-enter the community. From the last twenty years of observation, I admit that this ideal would be out of reach for some members, such as the very seriously paralyzed residents who did not have the physical health to live independently. But I also understood that though their body was paralyzed, their brain still worked. That's the most important thing. I trust that with their brain they can still learn a skill according to their physical condition and maybe by the end they still can look after themselves, financially at least.

We are only half way there; the quadriplegics still depend on others' help for their daily routine.

They could not fly off with their own wings as they wished.

For these people I have to look for alternative solutions such as providing for them a new Maison Chance where they can stay as long as they need. They will feel more secure as they get older. But I do not wish to build an old people's home, so I was thinking of modifying Maison Chance to accommodate several generations living and helping one another, like the old extended family.

The main problem for this project was to be able to find suitable jobs for the handicapped when they get older. Some simple jobs that the elderly could do would be to read stories for children at bed time, to teach them how to use the computers or read and write to the illiterate. But in general, older people like gardening, enjoying the calm and quiet environment to feel closer to nature. So, maybe caring for potted plants would please them and we could build them low work benches to pot the cuttings.

This project requires a large piece of land, so I looked all around but I could not find one. Land in our village of Binh Hung Hoa was getting more expensive.

About the same time, a disabled woman contacted me saying she wished to build a center for the elderly disabled in Da Lat, the city center of Lam Dong District. This region is about 5,000 feet above sea level. I went to Da Lat to meet her. It was in the winter, so it was cold, and I realized this weather is not suitable for the disabled as most of them have arthritis. Da Lat itself is on a hilltop and the roads are mostly hilly and difficult for wheelchairs to maneuver. After studying the location, I also found out that there are already a few charities operating there, so I started looking elsewhere.

The most suitable location has to meet two conditions: It could not be in a mountain area and it should be without any other social services. This would help my new project of caring for the elderly disabled as well as the local unfortunates.

I was looking first at the land near the border of Cambodia, but the people in this area are quite well off. They came to settle here for business from different regions. I continued my search for the ideal location.

Also, for easy administration and management the new place should not be more than a day trip from Saigon so that the residents of Maison Chance Saigon could visit easily or could spend their holidays there for a change of air. The members who love gardening or caring for animals could move there as well.

Another important point to be considered is how to convince the sponsors to support a project for Maison Chance in the country? To construct the building is one thing but to maintain it another matter and the convenience in transportation and communications with headquarters is another essential condition for maintaining the project's operations.

For a while now I have heard about the use of horses in physiotherapy for paralyzed patients with back pain. It would be interesting to use these animals as a mode of transportation as well. We could use animal therapy to help patients to recover and at the same time create a tourist attraction for those who like sightseeing on horseback in a wilderness not yet touched by human hands.

## *Freddy and the Land Inspection Trips*

For two years, I went to inspect 15 different locations for our new project. To keep a photographic record of these trips, I usually invited our photographer Freddy to come with me. Freddy, who came from Switzerland, was both photographer and agriculturalist. He visited Maison Chance for the first time in 2005 when we were building the Take Wing Center. He asked us politely if he could take some photographs. I liked Freddy and, besides his passion for photography, he was also interested in the life of the agricultural peasants and the hermit artists. Like me, he loved to observe what was happening in his surroundings. We became good friends and Freddy accompanied me in some of these land inspection trips. He visited Vietnam two or three time a year and whenever he came we made these crazy trips together.

We went to Gia Lai and Kontum, near the Laotian border where some land for the project was offered to us. We tried to visit some local charities hoping to find one to be the local partner with Maison Chance. Along the Central Highland there used to be some Christian friars who supported the minority population. This location I also found unsuitable for our purposes; it is too far from Saigon and the roads are bad.

Besides the two places in the Central Highland, we also went to visit Lam Dong District and its central city Bao Loc. This time, I took eight of my teenage children with me, so they could see the living conditions of the poor outside Maison Chance. Two of the boys were brought to Maison Chance by the local police, however they were not the first people accompanied by the police to Maison Chance. Others were victims of sexual abuse, of brutality, or individuals whose usefulness was over, so they were now abandoned. Without any solution, the police brought them to Maison Chance hoping they could be reformed. The police had faith in us, because in the end we could demonstrate that we are effective in dealing with the problems. But for our part we had to call for the police to help when we could not discipline some residents ourselves. Thành, for example, was a quarrelsome boy so I asked a couple of police officers to come to Maison Chance in their jeep and threaten to take him away. Thành calmed down quickly and behaved properly again.

In Bao Loc, we visited the center managed by the religious sisters who were caring for the mentally retarded. As we came in I was surprised to see Thành's face light up as he immediately recognized Sister Oanh, the sister-in-charge. She also recognized Thành, but she said she only knew him as Hung and she did not know why we called him Thành, a different name.

She told me about Thành. Over 25 years ago, during the last few years of the 1980's, Thành lived in the orphanage run by these sisters in Saigon, but when he turned ten he had to move out according to the house rules. So, the 'good ones' were moved to Bao Loc for agricultural work and the rest, including Thành, had to go to the Psychiatric Center at Thu Duc.

That was the place where I first met Thành. It was the worst time of his life; a nightmare of living among the mental ill and the lunatics. Thành was badly treated and by the end of his stay his loneliness was his only company. When he left the center, he could not even remember his own name.

Bao Loc Center, the nuns' facility we were visiting, was government owned. The residents here were all cared for with jobs provided in gardening, tea harvesting or caring for domesticated animals.

The lightly disabled were very proud of their achievement here. We joked that this place was ideal for Thành, so he should stay back. But he declined even though he was happy to catch up with the old sister.

After that we stopped by another orphanage on the road from Saigon to Da Lat at the bottom of the Madagui Pass. There were not enough job opportunities at this place and the roads were treacherous and caused many injuries to the disabled. This center could only offer the minimum services to the residents and there were no other activities at all. The Director of the Orphanage complained that they hardly had any visitors because the location was not very convenient to manage or to drop by.

This place reminded me of how important it is to offer different attractions to tempt the tourists.

Horses alone were not enough. What about the elephants living somewhere in Vietnam? Elephants are intelligent, sensitive and huge in size. Even though they still exist, there is a danger that they could become extinct here.

On the way back to Saigon we stopped at Dak Lak, a mountainous region in the Central Highlands where there are numerous elephants. We visited a few social services agencies here. I noticed that among the residents, there were a lot of people with brain damage and they lived in deplorable conditions. Their severe handicaps make caring for them very difficult.

When I began Maison Chance I was particularly interested in the young children, the serious cases of paralysis, the elderly homeless, the deaf and the blind. However, a number of experienced social workers told me that I cannot take care of everyone and I should perhaps pay at attention to a couple of groups. It was so true; no one can be an expert in many fields. Each field required a complete understanding to make it a success. To help the less fortunate, I had to learn the needs of each person.

I had decided on two main groups: the active disabled and disadvantaged children. They were all intelligent people and they can be educated culturally and vocationally. The aim of Maison Chance is to help them to fly away with their own set of wings, so that they do not depend on us all their lives.

I have to work out a long-term solution for a number of elderly disabled residents of Maison Chance. However, another idea occurred to me: Why I should I not use this opportunity to help the mentally challenged as well?

## *The Official Birth of the Krong No Project*

After looking at all the possibilities to start the new project, I consulted Google Maps to find the way to Krong No Hamlet in Dak Nong District. This was the only place in the Central Highland District that has no social services for the disadvantaged. I marked the location and prepared to go for a visit to Krong No.

At Buon Choah (Village Choah) I met Y Bar and his wife H'Nhac of the Ede tribe. They live in a wooden hut with their two children, but the surroundings of their humble dwelling were as beautiful as a fairy tale. Giant petrified lava stones formed a spectacular wall and Y Bar grew corn in between the stones. His wife—the mother of their young children—suffered from a serious heart condition but they could not afford to have her operated on, so she slowly deteriorated.

At Nam Nung Hamlet, we met Su, a young man from a Thai tribe that migrated down from the North. He was lying on the floor and his continuing convulsions caused his mouth to distort and his body to twist. Most of his muscles had atrophied and he could not talk. Su had suffered convulsions like these for the last four months but prior to that he was a strong, healthy person.

A picture of Su and his wife on their wedding day hung on the wall. His wife now stood next to us crying, while on one arm she carried her new-born baby and with the other hand she fed her husband.

They had been married for only one year.

Not far from Hamlet Nam, on an isolated hill in the hamlet of N'Dir, lived a group of the white Dao tribe; they also migrated here from North Vietnam after the big floods. Here I met Chung, a young man who was born a cripple. His world was within the four walls of his hut. We offered him a wheelchair and pushed him out of the hut. It was the first time he had seen the blue sky.

Here people are very poor, and they live on the cassava, corn and coffee crops. And there is not much mentionable beautiful scenery except for a few falls on the river Serepok, the only river in Vietnam that does not run into the Pacific Ocean. Its source is in Krong No and it runs up to the northwest before entering Cambodia.

I wanted to find out more about the waterfalls north of Krong No. The almost four-and-a-half-mile paved road runs through virgin forests and is being watched by the forest inspectors.

A waterfall is one of Gia Long's natural wonders, but it is still in its wilderness state and tourism has not discovered it yet. This waterfall is about 50 feet high and its water pours into a lake bordered by petrified lava stones. The crystal clear blue water is edged by giant forest trees which attract thousands of blue and yellow butterflies. This is indeed a magic place.

In 1930, Ex-Emperor Bao Dai visited this area and was so impressed with its natural beauty that he started the foundation for a hanging bridge, however this project was left unfinished.

I had a hunch that this would be the right place for my new project. This is also an ideal habitation for keeping our elephants. They can feed themselves in the forests while drinking and bathing where the rivers meet, and they would be protected against poachers. Imagine the sight of elephants bathing and playing with the children and visitors, so peaceful and so joyful.

Maybe our new Center would be bigger and better equipped to welcome hundreds of disadvantaged people. We will teach animal husbandry for raising poultry, fish and we will breed Phu Quoc dogs. We will have our own vegetable gardens to supply our residents, and if they over produced they could use their surplus for a source of extra income. For the gardening and the animal husbandry we will choose the right residents, young people with physical health. The elderly and the disabled could also join in, according to their own ability. We will construct an area suitable for the handicapped in wheelchairs.

We would build separate bungalows for visitors who appreciate natural beauty, enjoy sightseeing on horseback and would like to be friends with the residents.

All buildings would only be on one floor, so the construction would not interfere with the landscape and would be more suitable for wheelchair users.

......................................................

*Tim pushing the wheelchair on a walk (at Dak Nong)?*

I have loved animals since I was a child when I had many animal friends. I like all animals, but I am very partial to horses; they are such intelligent and magnificent animals. However, I have never met an elephant except in circuses or in zoos or even though books.

At ten, I had the opportunity to do illustrations for a children's magazine on wild animals. Through this work I realized all animals could be extinct one day. I drew so many animals, including elephants and other endangered animals. I felt sorry for their fate, but I never dreamt that I was as passionate about protecting them as I was at this moment.

Near 30 years later, I met my first elephant in the Central Highlands. They have a pitiful life. In the morning they take tourists sightseeing in a heavy frame constructed of bamboo and tied to the elephant's body. Afterwards, they pull giant logs of wood from the forest. Men abuse these elephants and they are constantly in chains. The animals are prevented from natural reproduction in order to maintain the continuity of the species.

The relationship between man and elephant is very complex. It is a circular question with no final solution. Men exploit the forest for wood, depriving the elephants of their food. So, elephants have to look for food elsewhere often raiding field crops and farm buildings. Then men eliminate the elephants by netting them or poisoning them, so in return the elephants pay them back by attacking the men.

To solve this problem, we have to do more than just to protect the elephants. We have to make sure that we understand the importance of the survival of the species. Men must learn to protect their crops while at the same time thinking of the survival of the last 200 elephants left in Vietnam.

I had learned a bit about the elephants, the different species and the regions where they live. Even though it was the first time I had met elephants I felt I could talk to them while stroking them gently.

Touching the elephants give me the strong feeling of how small we are; next to them we are nothing and I suddenly knew that the elephant has the upper hand. I always feel something special when I am near this animal. It brings me a special kind of happiness, a natural healing power for even the healthy people.

I believe that caring for the animals is caring for human kind, because humans and animals co-exist with other beings on this planet and we need to help one another to survive.

It was time for some concrete work.

I made an appointment to see the Dak Nong authority at Gia Nghia to present my new social project. The assistant chairperson of the People's Committee responsible for the district social services was enthusiastic about my proposal. In every meeting, her sympathetic support showed in her smiling face.

I asked them to grant me a piece of land next to the water fall and they agreed and granted to Maison Chance a piece of land of just under 1,400 square yards to construct the first purpose-built social services complex in the region.

........................................................

After more than twenty years, now I truly understand the saying, "a drop of water in the ocean, a grain of sand in the desert" or, more correctly, "a grain of rice in the bowl of a starving person."

I will continue with my work that I started. There are so many projects awaiting me. Up to now I have spent more time in Vietnam than I was in Switzerland. I was born in Switzerland, but I became an adult in Vietnam, my second country. This land taught me work ethics. It also taught me how to sacrifice your personal life to better the life of the less fortunate. I will go on until my last breath, but I pray that Maison Chance will continue on even after I am gone.

To guarantee its long-term survival, I have to make my Maison Chance officially a social services agency of Vietnam, an independent organisation. I had been searching for a solution for the last few years. The only solution is for me to become a Vietnamese citizen.

After many nights lying awake thinking about it, I decided to submit my application to become naturalized Vietnamese. After one year and nine months of waiting, I received a letter from the President of Vietnam agreeing for Rebeaud Aline to become a naturalized Vietnamese citizen. My new name is Hoang Nu Ngoc Tim or "The Princess with a Precious Heart".

*"I love animals."*

....................................................

Basically, not much has changed. I am still Tim and I still live in an extended family known as Maison Chance. I share my life with the orphans and the serious handicapped. Their names are Lanh, Trung, Hao, Khanh, Thành, An, Tien, and Hai.

We meet at night, and as their adopted mother, I listen to the stories of my children and in turn I tell them about my day. I explain things which they don't understand and answer any questions they might ask. I teach them cooking so one day they can become good cooks and make me special dishes.

That is my family and it is exactly like any other family.

We have over ten Phu Quoc dogs, a special breed with special hair curls on their back and web feet like the duck so they are good swimmers. They are extremely intelligent, fast runners and they can jump very high. We have to watch them carefully, so they cannot escape into the streets where they could be taken and killed for meat. My young children are responsible for the dogs since I like to start the youngsters with small responsibilities before giving them serious work.

This morning was the morning of the 15 of July (Lunar Calendar). When I was writing the last pages of this book, I saw my children standing on the first floor throwing down josh (pagoda) money for the forgotten lonely ghosts. This is a tradition of the Vietnamese; they are Buddhists and follow the lunar calendar. In the middle of the July lunar calendar is an event similar to the Western All Souls Day. On that day, people offer food and incense for the lonely forgotten souls who do not have any close friends or family. No one teaches the kids these traditions but they all know to practice from life experiences. And this is unique in Eastern culture.

My story is not finished and if I continue writing it then it will never be finished.

My warmest thanks to all who work with us and who, help us at Maison Chance. I could not achieve anything on my own.

Thanks to the help and support of our sponsors, thousands of people who are less fortunate than us have found a new spark of life. There are so many of you it is impossible to name everyone in this book, but I will never forget them.

And to return to the beginning, I have written this to share with you what I believe. If love is an infectious disease, then I hope this book will help me to bring this love to hundreds of readers.

I found the meaning of life through my work, through sharing my life with others and I believe that an action, no matter how small, from each and every one of us would contribute to the happiness of others.

*A Vovinam class held by Vietnamese volunteers at Take Wing Center.*
*Vovinam is a popular Vietnamese martial art.*

# Real Life Stories

# Kim Van Phuoc

*"I am a lucky man, I have two mothers. I dearly love my birth mother as much as my adopted mother. She is Mother Tim, who had brought me up and helped me to become a good person."*

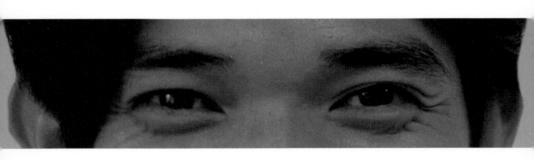

At present my family lives in a rented apartment at Village Chance. I feel very proud of myself whenever I look at our wedding photos. To me my wife is a beautiful lady. When I got married Mother Tim took care of all the arrangements from A to Z for the wedding, the most important event of my life. Mother Tim was there on behalf of my parents, looking gorgeous in her traditional Vietnamese *ao dai*.

When my wife was with our first child, we were broke. Again, it was Mother Tim who came to the rescue. She always reminds us to take care of ourselves and stay healthy.

Thanks to the assistance and encouragement of my adopted mother, we now have two nice boys.

My birth mother is mentally ill. Before she had me, she was a wanderer; she went here and there and sometimes she was absent for months on end. Then one day she came back not knowing that she was with child, me. She was so frightened that she would not dare to say who the father of the child was when my grandmother and my uncle questioned her.

A month after she gave birth to me my mother wandered off again, leaving me to grow up with my grandmother and my eldest brother's family. We were very poor. By the time I was six, my two cousins and I sold lottery tickets to help our family. Every day we went from street to street, from hostel to hostel in downtown Saigon trying to ply our trade. But it was not that easy, we had to face with being humiliated, cursed, chased off and sometimes even beaten up.

One day when I was over tired, I fell asleep in the corner of a hostel. When I awoke I discovered that all my tickets and money had been stolen. Unfortunately, on that same day, my two cousins lost all theirs gambling.

When we returned my uncle was furious and he could not control his anger. He hung us upside down and beat us up. I could not understand the logic why should I get punished when someone else stole my money and my tickets? I remember the heavy blows; my cousin was so frightened that he pissed in his pants. I decided to run away: first to avoid the heavy blows and second, I resented the unfair punishment.

By the time I was nine I lived on the streets. When I was hungry I went to the back of a hostel waiting for the food leftover by the residents. When I was exhausted I slept under a tree or an awning sometimes. From the kids of other districts, especially District One where there are many luxurious hotels and foreign tourists, I learned how to help open and close taxi doors to get some tips. Once I was lucky; a generous man gave me a 100,000 Dong tip (roughly 4.40 US dollars) but that did not happen often.

It was a hard life, but I had to go on and to keep on fighting; nothing frightened me anymore. I did not think of tomorrow or my future, which was just something too far away and vague. One day, while wandering around the hostels in District One on Pham Ngu Lao Street, I ran into Mother Tim. At first, I thought she was just another European tourist on this popular street. But when she asked me if I'd like to have a roof over my head and food in my belly, I asked myself the same question.

Of course, the dream of every street kid is to have somewhere to live and food to eat. But I wondered why this foreign lady took particular notice of me. What did she want from me, I kept asking myself? However, I had enough of this hostile environment, so I decided to follow her home to the outer suburb where the orphans and the local community called her home Maison Chance (Lucky House).

So, my life turned over to a new page. New clothing to replace the old rags. I was given exercise books to go to school, and I managed to learn the alphabet. At the beginning I did not feel comfortable at the house because I was so used to my own routine; I had slept wherever and whenever it suited me. Here everything was different; there were rules to be followed. It was difficult to know and then I met Dien, another street kid rescued by Mother Tim. Dien wished to go back living on the streets, so Dien and I decided to run away together.

When Mother Tim discovered my escape, she took a motorbike taxi to chase after me, but I was faster. However, after a few days back on the streets, I was starving and exhausted. I returned to Maison Chance.

Again, I refused to go to school. I was one of the most stubborn boys at Maison Chance then. I would not study, so during the holidays I was not allowed to play with my friends and I had to catch up with my homework.

Mother Tim even had a tutor to help me studying but it was of no use; I was as bad as ever. Mother Tim was very angry and forced me to study. I was mad and went on a hunger strike and that worried Mother Tim a great deal, but she did not know that I always ate rice cake when she was away. Nothing worries me except for sadness, therefore I apologized to Mother Tim and I did not wish to see her sad. Even now I still remember this episode and I feel in debt to her. If Mother Tim had not punished me, I would not be educated and would not be a good person. I am now a painter.

Mother Tim arranged everything for my wedding and after the wedding I left the painting room at Maison Chance to work at a factory. But the job was boring compared to the lively jobs of the street vendors, so we bought a large quantity of clothing and started our street stall. But this job was much more complicated than we had thought; money did not grow on trees.

One day while I was working at the street stall, Mother Tim walked past. She was so surprised to see me all skin and bones, covered with dust and sweaty. She suggested that I come should come back home. I remember my mixed feeling of joy and happiness, tinted with feeling of shame. I had disobeyed my Mother Tim.

I quickly tried to sell off my goods to return to Maison Chance, and this story I will never forget.

At present I live in Village Chance, a special facility reserved for people in wheelchairs. Since I am a disadvantaged orphan, I am allowed to share this accommodation and to help the disabled in their daily lives. My wife works in the sewing room at the Take Wing Center and I studied the making of patisseries. I became the first trained and experienced baker at the bakery room in Village Chance. I have two lovely boys; the older is two and a half and each time he sees Mother Tim he runs into her arms and gives kisses to his "Ba Noi" (paternal grandmother).

Have you seen the older lady who does the cleaning around the Village Chance courtyard? She is my birth mother. I found her a few years back and I brought her back here to live with us. Mother Tim gave her a cleaning job at Village Chance. Now that she is employed, and she has her grandsons with her, her mental state is much more balanced.

I am not rich, but I have a roof over my head and a family. A family with two loving mothers, a good wife and two nice boys. My future is assured.

# Ly Thi Bich Lien

*"When the doctor told me that my disease was incurable, due to the long term untreated spinal tuberculosis, I could only cry and plead with them that I would rather die on the operating table than slowly wither on the sick bed."*

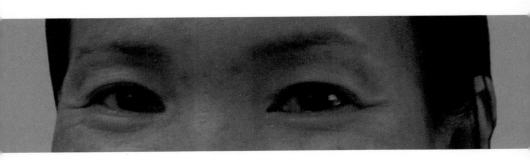

My name is Lien. I was born into a war-torn country and life then was very hard, especial for a big family like mine. My parents gave birth to nine children. I am the youngest and I always feel proud to believe that mine was a happy family.

I was born and bred in Phan Thiet where the sand is white. Most of the people there depend on the fishing industry for their living. My parents built a small house on the land owned by my grandmother. They did not have enough money to buy bricks for the walls, even after they tried to save up for a long time, so we ended up with mud and straw walls. Both materials come from nature and they are very common in this region. We only added on the kitchen and the pigsty a few years later.

My mother was a street vendor; she sold sweet soups to support us. Every day at the crack of dawn the whole family got up and give her a hand to get ready. While she was cooking in the kitchen, my father had to shred 15 coconuts and each of my siblings was given a different task. Being the youngest I was exempted from this chore; my main task was to study and occasionally I was asked to dust the furniture or clean the table.

As the sun was up my mother was already on her way with a heavy load at each end of the bamboo pole on her shoulder. She plied her trade from street to street. While my siblings walked to schools by themselves, I was the only one to be taken to school by my father. We had to dodge the stray bullets many times; we were still at war.

My father, unlike other men, was nice and gentle; he had never hurt his wife or children. And as for my mother, I cried whenever I remembered her nodding off next to her sweet soup baskets waiting for customers. I understood that to care for us she had no time to sleep and I felt even sadder.

It was quite strange that all the memories of my family were related the longan tree in the front of our house. My father bought the seedling from Hue and it turned out to be an excellent tree. It was a big tree like a giant umbrella and very prolific and delicious. We always prayed for strong winds during the season, so we could eat until our belly ached from the fruits on the grounds. And under this tree so many family portraits were taken on special occasions. They were simple, small black and white photographs but now I treasure them as my precious belongings.

When I was seven, my family decided to move to the new economic zone at Tanh Linh since there were so many of us and we had run into financial problems. I was the youngest and still at school, so I was left boarded with the family of my aunt and uncle.

Three years later, when I was in grade five, my family was in a big crisis; my father became sick and his health deteriorated fast. When we managed to raise enough money to take him to see the doctor, it was too late. He was at stage four of cancer of the liver and there was not much hope.

My mother worked even harder to pay for my father's medical care and she made frequent trips to the Delta cities to buy goods in demand in the mountains. At the same time, my sister could not do much to help since she had just given birth to her child. So, most family chores were given to me, a young girl of ten.

I felt both sad and a bit self-conscious when I remember my school days. I was the smallest in class, so I was always in the front row and it was always troublesome to find something decent to wear. I ended up trying to borrow pieces of clothing from friends.

When my aunt found out she offered me some hand-me-downs from her son. They were clothing for boys, but I did not care even though I knew my friends laughed at me for wearing boys' clothes. Fortunately, there was no school uniform then.

My elder sister felt sorry for me. She was once in tears telling me, "We have no money, father is sick, mother works day and night and there is not enough money to cover for father's medication. And here I am the eldest sister and I can't afford some clothes for you. I am so sorry." I thought my eldest sister was much older than me, so she saw things differently from me, because to me that time was not that bad.

Then it was time for my father to leave us forever. I was asleep then, but I was told my father called out my name before he died.

After the funeral, we moved back to the new economic zone in the mountains. I left school before finishing grade five. I changed my city life for a harsh life in the dense forests; a peasant's life without electricity, working in the muddy fields from dawn to dusk for the annual crops. This was my life until I was 16. My siblings got married and in turn left, by the end only my mother and I were left at home to fend for ourselves.

Other late teenage girls were coquettish, and they liked to make themselves pretty, but not me. I was too focused on making a living to think of this natural instinct. Every day I helped my mother at the market and with any spare time I went to collect wood in the forests with other friends or I tended to my vegetable garden.

Life then was very harsh, as if it was predestined and everything was in the hands of God. When the monsoon rain came, it turned the road into a muddy, slippery mess with footprints left by people and buffalos. There was no other mode of transport than walking and even then, I had to learn to roll up my trousers to my knees and then secure them carefully with string to keep them out of the mud. I also had to take off my shoes to successfully maneuver the muddy, slippery road. When the flash floods rushed down from the mountains, this road became a fast running river and the water could rise up to my chest. So, I had to carry the goods basket on my head as I slowly followed the road to get to the market safely.

One day when a flash flood came rushing down the creeks bringing with it a lot of firewood, my sister-in-law and I went to collect the wood at the lower end of the creek. It was the custom of this region to harvest natural resources the easy way and the flood water saved us from dragging the logs through tortuous, bumpy and long roads down from the forest.

I had done this many times before, but this time when I tried to get up with the heavy logs secured to the bamboo pole on my shoulder, I could not manage to stand up on my legs.

My health deteriorated visually. I still could get around on my feet though, but I kept going downhill in spite of all the cures and the medication.

Four months later, one day when waking up I tried to get out of bed, but as soon as I took a few steps, I fell down. The pain felt like a thousand knife cuts through my flesh and my bones. I remember the exact date when this happened; it was October 18, 1985. My family had to borrowed money from everyone and my mother had to sell her house to pay for my cure, but without any result. In desperation, my family even found a shaman to exorcise the ghost that resided in my body and was destroying me.

Day after day and month after month, I lay waiting for death. I could only be in one position on my belly, my spinal cord swelled up and my both of my legs shrank toward the front because they were left untreated by a physiotherapist for a long time. Due to my staying in one position, I had a lot of bedsores on my body. Every day with the help of a mirror I tried to clean and dress these sores myself using cotton wool soaked in an alum water solution. The sores were pus-filled and disgusting to look at, so I took care of them myself rather than making someone else do it.

I lived on two meals a day of rice and porridge with some dried fish that my mother saved from her market day to feed the family. For eight long years I lived in this desperation. Every time I held my bowl of rice in my hand, tears filled my eyes. When left on my own, I screamed out loud to cleanse myself of all my suppressed sadness and desperation.

One day, among a pile of old newspapers my mother bought to wrap her dried fish, there was a copy of that day's newspaper.

I remember it was *Nguoi lao dong* (The Laborer) newspaper and it had a health column with an article about tuberculosis of the spinal cord. I read this article and I asked my friend to take some photos of my condition. I then sent a letter with the photos to the Orthopaedic Trauma Center. I only did that as the last resort and I did not expect a response from them.

However, I could not stop crying with happiness four days later when I received a reply from the Center saying that, due to my circumstances, they agreed to treat me free of charge! The letter, which I still treasure after more than 20 years, was signed by Nurse Truc Mai.

That night, my brother managed to borrow 50,000 dong (US $2.20) from the neighbor to take me to the hospital where we waited impatiently for the results of the tests. Once again, I was thrown back into the depths of my desperation when the doctor informed me that my Pott disease was beyond treatment because the tuberculosis of the vertebrae had been left untreated for a long time.

Hearing this, my tears rained down on my face. I pleaded with the doctors to grant me a chance; I'd rather die on the operating table than to slowly waste away in my sick bed. By the end, moved by my tearful pleadings, the doctors agree to give me a chance to live. I was treated and given aftercare at the hospital for two years with no fee. They operated on my vertebrae to rebuild my wasted legs; the leg joints and muscles had shrunken and deformed while being immobile for a long time.

Every operation was successful but still I could not use my legs. For the more than two years I spent at the hospital, my mother worked even harder to make a living and to help in my daily care. She hardly had time to visit me and one of my young nephews nursed me through.

Then one day, a young foreign lady with chestnut brown hair and beautiful smile visited the hospital and she was particularly interested in the poor and neglected patients including me. When she learned of my unfortunate life she agreed to let me move to Maison Chance where I would be looked after. I was then told she was Mother Tim.

A few days later, I was discharged from the Center with a bundle of possessions. I took a motorcycle taxi to go to my new home and as the old driver took me through many quiet, winding roads, my mind was busy with impatient expectation. He finally stopped in front of an old house in Binh Hung Hoa District.

Maison Chance was then an old house that Tim rented to share with a few orphans and disabled persons. Life was a struggle in those days and every expense required to look after us depended solely on Tim's family in Switzerland. Our material life was very poor, but our family life together was rich. Each of us had some daily job, either keeping the floor cleaned or washing dirty dishes, and this daily life bonded us together like a real family.

Every night the whole family, including the orphans and the disabled in wheelchairs, shared a simple meal of rice and fish amid an animated atmosphere. We talked and joked about everything and anything like any other family. Tim lived and ate with us and participated in every family activity. The disabled in wheelchairs got physiotherapeutic treatment daily and we all were educated in basic knowledge. Tim taught us painting since she was originally a painter.

After dinner we sat around playing a guitar and singing to amuse ourselves. As for me, I chose to be trained in sewing and painting. However, most of my time was spent in the kitchen since I love cooking.

Communal life was complicated due to the fact that we were all complete strangers gathered together to live under the roof of Maison Chance. Conflicts were unavoidable sometimes; however, they were quickly resolved. At times, we had family members who behaved so badly that they caused unhappiness all around and this could cause Tim to get angry. Seeing her face getting red with anger frightened me, even though I knew it was not my fault. I tried my best to avoid her, so if I saw her entering the front door, I rolled my wheelchair through the back door. However, after a few days, Tim was back to normal, happy and loving. She usually approached the guilty party to show them not only what was wrong with their behavior and attitudes but also to demonstrate her care and love for them.

But this was nothing compared to the misery that the disabled in wheelchairs experienced when the monsoon rains came. Our house was below the road level, so we had water half way up the wheels of our chairs. The road from Maison Chance to the market was flooded and full of potholes, and we had to take turns going to the market.

Unfortunately for me, at that time I was the only female among the residents, so I had to go to the market more often than most. To keep the rain and mud off of the food and me, I completely covered over the wheelchair with my raincoat, and I wrapped my legs with two large plastic bags to keep them off the stinky, dirty flood water. The trip to the market was therefore strenuous and time consuming. But coming back loaded with bags piled over my lap while hanging onto my chair armrests as well as onto the foot rest was even more difficult.

Time passed, and I was getting used to my new life. My mother came to visit whenever she saved up enough money for the train ticket. I also found the love of my life at Maison Chance. I fell in love with Hung, who came to Maison Chance after me. He was the victim of a train accident when his spinal cord was damaged, and he became a paraplegic. We shared the same physical problem as well as other life challenges and this brought us much closer together.

After ten years living at Maison Chance, we both finished our training, so we left Maison Chance to make room for others less fortunate. Like other "flown-from-the-nest" members, we looked for a room to share in a boarding house near the Take Wing Center. It was a hard life to live in these rented rooms. Not only were they not designed for wheelchair users, but they also were flooded regularly during the rainy season. We spent many sleepless nights cleaning.

Luckily in 2010, Miss Tim was successful in raising enough funds to build a village with accommodations suitable for wheelchair users; it is called Village Chance. Many "flown-from-the-nest" members of Maison Chance like us came back to the village to live together again. Even though we have to pay a nominal rent to live here, we are very happy living in a separate apartment specifically designed for wheelchair access. From the kitchen to the bathroom everything is designed to suit our needs.

To continue my own love story with Hung, after six months living together at Village Chance, thanks to a benefactor, we managed to organize our small wedding at the Village. It was a cozy wedding party attended by all members of Maison Chance. After 15 years of sharing our love, we are now enjoying our complete happiness.

At present we live together happily at Village Chance and we work daily at the sewing room at Take Wing Center where I also run a small stall selling goods for students at the canteen. We come home at night to our daily life together, but every now and then we feel anxious about our health since we are both very frail. And since we have damaged spinal cords, we missed out on the joy of parenthood.

I always remember to thank God, and those who gave us the chance of a happy life. And it is not until now that I have truly found the spring of my life.

# Nguyen Hoang Thuong

*"As time passed, I felt more relaxed in my new environment. My life improved considerably compared to my old life in the country. Mother Tim had never beaten me, on the contrary, she healed my wounds, loved and cared for me."*

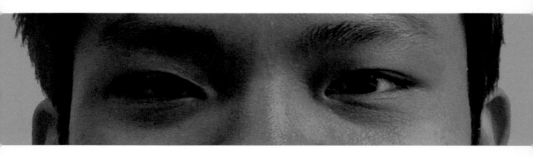

My name is Thuong, I was born in 1988 in Dong Nai, a province north of Saigon, and in Vietnamese, my name means "Love and Care." A few months after my birth bad omens foretold my future; my mother died of cancer when I was only three months old. My father was not with us when I was born and until now I still don't know who my father is. I was without any relatives. At the hospital a family took pity on me and handed me over to a lady who had already adopted a little orphan girl. I spent my first few years growing up in Dong Nai. Even though I had a family I was not really cared for properly; my adopted mother and sister were away most of the day working and they returned late at night.

I ended up looking after myself most of the time. My adopted mother had to farm the fish to sell them at the market. She did enroll me in the local school, but she did not really pay any attention to my schooling and slowly I became a bad boy. I preferred running around in the streets to sitting in the classroom. I spent a lot of time on my own without any friends and slowly I was completely isolated from the community.

My adopted mother worked very hard during the day and she returned home at night she was very tired, so any small problems could make her angry. She expressed her anger by beating me with a knotted rope, even though I was only a little boy and what I did was nothing serious. I felt the pain each time the knotted rope hit me. My sister was luckier than me since she did not suffer the beatings.

My adopted mother was not rich by any means, but she could give us all we needed daily. But one day for no reason, all the fish in the pond died and so we ran into difficulty financially. Luckily my mother was a clever business woman and she started the fish farm again with new stock. We also installed a warning machine for the fish to swim into a protected area when the weather was bad.

One day in a heavy downpour, I ran out to the pond and tried to move the warning machine out of the rain. In a hurry my foot touched the hot motor of the machine and my foot was severely burnt. It was so painful that I could only cry, and I could not even put my foot down. I was nine years old then.

My mother could not take me to the hospital then and after a few days the burn became so severe that nothing could be done. My mother could not do anything to help. Luckily, a priest learnt of our circumstance and introduced me to Maison Chance where I would be cared for and where I could live with others who suffered the same unlucky life as myself. The priest took me to Mother Tim's house in 1997.

At the beginning, life at Maison Chance was very difficult for me. I was a shy, alone boy and in this big home I did not have any friends. I cried often and wished my mother would turn up and take me home. I was much darker than the city children at Maison Chance, so they nicknamed me "Den" (Black) and others also called me "Cameroon". They did not intend to be cruel; it was only a name solely because my skin was darker than everybody else in the house.

I often thought of my birth mother and I wished one day I would find out what she looked like. In fact, I had no memory of my birth mother, not even the maternal scent or her facial features. I often wondered if I looked like my mother and questioned where my dark skin came from.

As time passed, I felt more comfortable with my new environment; my new life was definitely better than my country existence. Mother Tim had never beaten me; on the contrary she healed my wound, loved and cared for me. I kept in contact with my first adopted mother, however the distance kept us apart and we only managed to catch up with each other every two or three years.

When I first arrived at Maison Chance I was almost illiterate. I learned a few letters in the alphabet; for example, I could distinguish only the letter "p" from the letter "a". I continued my education at Maison Chance and I immediately attended the French language course. By the time I was seventeen, I graduated from the training course and I worked in the artisan room at The Take Wing Center. I did not enjoy this job.

Mother Tim sent me to be trained outside in designing web sites. When I finished this short course, I could help in some administrative duties at the Take Wing Center. However, I got bored sitting in the office all day in front of the computer; my legs were for walking I reasoned.

Finally, I became passionate about bar tending after a course at Saigon Tourist, and the social workers at Maison Chance helped me wholeheartedly to follow my new direction. They enrolled me into a well-known Australian non-profit hospitality school KOTO (Know One Teach One) for less fortunate street kids. I loved this course; as a small boy at Maison Chance I always helped in preparing our family meals. I really loved doing this job and I began reading cook books greedily.

I had my hair cut and donned my black uniform, discarding my long hair and colored shirts. I studied seriously, and I graduated with an A+.

After my graduation from KOTO, I had the chance to do my practical work with the best five-star hotels in central Saigon. I was trained at the Hotel Movenpick and the Hotel Caravelle. Later I was employed by the Hotel Hyatt and the Hotel Sheraton. However, I still prefer to cook at the Village Chance restaurant. It is my turn to help Mother Tim. But naturally my aim is to become a great chef and own my own restaurant one day.

# Tran Van Quang

*"Mother Tim did not approve of what I did but she did not abandon me. I kept repeating my bad behavior over and over and I do not know how Mother Tim coped with it. But one day it dawned on me that if I kept up with his bad behavior I would have no future."*

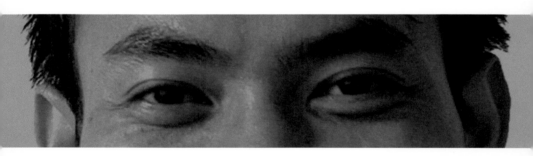

Quang is my name. Even today I still don't know who actually gave me this name. I don't even know when I was born and where was my home originally.

I remember as a child I lived in Hue near the Trang Tien Bridge. It was a good place for street kids who could survive there without too much trouble. There were always lots of passersby, and they mostly were foreign tourists who never finished their plates of food.

People told me that one day they saw two young men with a two or three-year-old boy coming down from the mountains. Then they saw the two men left without the little child. That little child was me, but I cannot say if this story is true since I was too little to know what was going on then.

When I was 15, I was watching a young foreign tourist eating. She must not have been very hungry because she did not finish her meal, so I approached and asked her for the left over. She did not want to give me the left over, but she ordered a new plate of food for me.

She spoke Vietnamese with a Southern accent, but I still understood. My first impression of this lady was that she was very nice and approachable. She wanted to know who I was and how I made my living, but I did not have much to tell her. She explained to me that she came from a faraway place where she has a house for the unfortunate orphans like me. After a long chat, she asked me to go to the beach with her. The beach was only about nine miles from Hue and yet I had never been. When I saw the beach, I jumped in and enjoyed the sea immensely.

Her name was Tim. When she took me back to Hue, I asked her if I could go to her house where she took care of orphans like me. She agreed, and she explained to me that it would be a long trip, but I was not scared. She asked me to meet her the next morning at the front of the Hue Pedagogical University, where she stayed overnight. I was unable to express the emotion I felt then. I was so excited that I was two hours early for my appointment the next day.

The train left at seven o'clock and arrived in Saigon the next morning. We had a sleeping berth and I could use the berth to sleep. During this time the train from Hue to Saigon did not exceed about 22 miles per hour on coal power. The train smelled badly and shook noisily and so it was impossible to sleep, but later Miss Tim told me that the worst smell was from my farting excessively. Of course, the reason for my farting was my eating bad food.

However, the long journey finally ended when we reached Maison Chance. I spent the first few nights with Miss Tim and after that I shared the accommodations with the other kids in the common room. At the beginning I found it a bit difficult to participate in the life at Maison Chance. I was given vitamins as a supplement since I was smaller than other kids of the same age. I was not sick; I was just born small.

I loved going to school so that I could have a stable life and a better future. Slowly I blended in with the communal life and with my new siblings. I started addressing Miss Tim as Mother Tim like the others. Besides my general education, I also registered to be a player with the local football (soccer) team. We played well in many games and I was one of the best players on the team. I also went to the gym to improve my body. At that time, gyms were not popular and the gym I attended was not well equipped except for some weights, but still we had to queue up to get in. After going to the gym for a while, I put on weight and especially my muscles started to develop.

Mother Tim was very proud of my improvement not only in my physical health but also in my studies. At the final primary school examination organized by the Education Department, I had the highest score among 1,700 students.

Unfortunately, I was not perfect; gambling for money was my weakness. I left school after I finished my seventh year against the advice and encouragement of Mother Tim. However, she enlisted me to be trained as a silversmith at a precious stones factory. I was a good at this craft and showed some talent, but I was often in absentia as I spent time at the billiard table or gambling houses. Due to this problem I had to change my work places often, but finally I managed to become a silversmith.

When I just turned 18 I got a job in a prestigious precious stone factory in Saigon and I started earning my own living. I left Maison

House and rented a room nearby. I visited Mother Tim and my siblings sometimes and I even had enough money to get a present for Mother Tim; a durian, her favorite fruit.

Unfortunately, I was addicted to gambling. I won sometimes but I often lost, and I was in debt. I could not pay my debt sometimes and I was hassled by the debt collectors hired by the local gangster group. I heard that Mother Tim was going overseas for three weeks so I asked her to lend me her motorbike to get to my new job, which was a bit far from where I lived. Mother Tim let me have the bike and as soon as she was on the plane I rode her bike straight to the cash convertor to pay off my debt to the gangsters. When Mother Tim returned I did not have the bike to return to her.

Even though she did not approve of my bad behavior, she did not abandon me. And as I kept repeating the same mistake, I often wondered how could Mother Tim put up with me? One day, it dawned on me that if I did not change I would have no future. I made a deal with Mother Tim to let me to gamble once more to pay off my debts, but I was not allowed to gamble any longer after that. I took this last chance and with my good luck I met my future wife. She was a young beautiful lady who lived on the same street. I was then 24 years old.

My future wife and I truly loved each other, and we got married. Suddenly I was a grown up and mature person. Now we are running a seafood grill stall near Maison Chance. We have a daughter of six and a son of two years and I finally quit gambling.

This is my life story and it is different from other life stories. And of course, my life road would not be paved with rose petals if I had not asked for the left-over meal from that young foreign tourist at Trang Tien Bridge in Hue.

# Ly Thi Bich Tram

*"Since I was a child, I always dreamt that I would study hard and when I grew up I could contribute to the home where my family was supported during the worst times and where I was brought up to be a mature responsible person."*

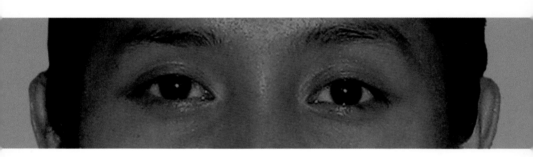

I am Tram. I was born in 1990 to a very poor family in Dong Nai Province. I was the second girl of a family of four daughters. My father was a laborer, and my mother was illiterate; she stayed at home to look after the family. My father was the only income earner, so we were extremely poor. When I was six my father was injured in a workplace accident and, because his spinal cord was crushed, he became a paraplegic. My youngest sister was less than a month old.

We had to sell our home and our land to pay for my father to go to the hospital. We therefore ran into severe financial difficulty. But luckily, we also ran into Mother Tim when she visited the hospital. When she learned of our difficult circumstance, she took my whole family back to Maison Chance to live with other disabled persons and orphans. My birth mother left us then, so my family burden fell squarely on Mother Tim's shoulders. She replaced our birth mother to bring us up and to educate us. Maison Chance was indeed the safe nest for our family of five and for other less fortunate persons.

Mother Tim not only gave us a roof over our heads, she gave us the chance to study and the loving care of a mother as well. Slowly I got over my sad lonely feeling. My sisters and I all attended school. In 2009, my second sister Giau got married. Mother Tim helped her to be trained as a hair dresser and she now has a son and a steady job. My next sister Tuyen was graduated as an accountant and in August 2014 she got married to a member of Maison Chance. Both work at the Take Wing Center. My youngest sister Uyen is studying to be a librarian. My father is still in his wheelchair and lives at Village Chance.

In 2009 I got a scholarship to study in the USA and this was when and where my new life direction began. I studied English for two years at Houston Community College in Houston, Texas. I studied during the week and worked on weekends to enrich my personal experience. Living in a foreign country, which I had never even dreamt of setting foot on ever, I found at first everything here different and unfamiliar.

Sometimes this new life became difficult and challenging, however I had never felt defeated. The challenges helped and encouraged me to be a better, more mature person. Here I also had the chance to meet up with the USA Maison Chance Foundation members for the first time.

In 2011 Mother Tim introduced me to Uncle David Duong Nguyen and Aunt Linh. Later on, I moved in with this family in Pennsylvania in the north of the USA, and here I had an extra elder sister, Van Ly, and a younger brother, Minh Thai.

Uncle David and his family treated me well. It was as if I was their own daughter and sibling. Uncle David and Aunt Linh taught me everything important about daily life, and they helped me with their wise advice and encouraged me to make progress in my studies. Here I began my course on Management and Development at Lehigh Community College.

Time flies. I was only a small child when I arrived at Maison Chance and I have lived and grown up there for the last 20 years among the love and support of the less fortunate. As a child, I dreamt that I would study hard and when I grew up I would be responsible and return to Maison Chance the support that it gave to my family when we were in desperate circumstances. I dreamt that would pay back all the hard work of bringing me up to be a mature good person.

My study lasted four long years in the USA and I graduated in December 2014. I had realized that during my life so far, I have received a lot of good luck and help from many people. After I graduated, I returned to Vietnam where there are so many more unfortunate people who are in need of help, and I began to realize my childhood dream of helping less fortunate people at Maison Chance where I grew up.

At present I work in the Project Office of Maison Chance.

Thank you, Maison Chance. Thank you, all the generous benefactors who have been supporting us.

# Dao Minh Phung

*"I lost everything at once. I had fallen into a dark hole of desperation and hopelessness. I often thought of killing myself. And I did try to meet death three times. But each time, my father interceded."*

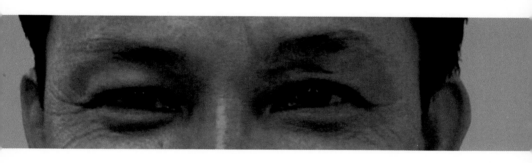

My name is Dao Minh Phung. I was born in 1967 to a poor family in Hue and all year round my parents worked the fields to support us. I have four siblings and when I was little, I herded the buffalo for my neighbor and I went to school in the afternoon. At that time, Central Vietnam was experiencing a severe famine and my family suffered badly; we did not have enough rice to eat daily. From then on, I was constantly troubled by the question of what could I do to prepare for my future?

I left school when I was 15 and continued my buffalo-herding job for my neighbor for another four years. For my living, I then spent two years in the army, followed by a stint of work in the forest. I chopped down trees and made coal to sell for my living.

I was married at 25 and a year later we had a son we named Vu. Unfortunately, when my son turned one, I had a bad accident working in the forest; a tree fell on top of me crushing my spinal cord. I could not get myself up, so my co-workers helped me and carried me home in a hammock where we arrived after 12 hours of walking through the dense forests.

They took me to Hue General Hospital. My mother fainted when she saw me, and she passed away a few months later from sadness. My father had to sell everything he owned, and we lived in the pagoda because we had nowhere else to go. My wife left me after the accident without even a goodbye and she took our son with her. I did not see my son for 16 years.

I lost everything at once. I had fallen into a dark hole of desperation and hopelessness. I often thought of killing myself. I did try to meet death three times, but each time my father interceded.

The accident took away my legs. I could not walk, and the unbearable pain came in waves torturing me. And the wound was badly infected and slowly became dead meat!

They transferred me to a Saigon hospital since no further treatment could be done for me in Hue. In Saigon I felt completely abandoned. The hospital discharged me since I could not pay the fee, so I ended up living homeless in the streets. I made my meager living selling lottery tickets.

My wounds were getting worse, and by the end I lost all my strength. I had a severe fever and I pleaded with the hospital to accept me. The nurses then transferred me to Room 212 where they kept all the paraplegics like me who had also lost their legs as well as their physical health. Tai and Minh were my first friends here and they were discharged from the hospital and left with a young lady; and that lady was Miss Tim. And when I was a bit better, Miss Tim also took me back to Maison Chance where I was cared for, and that was in 1996.

At that time Miss Tim did everything at Maison Chance. She cooked for us, took care of our wounds and educated us. I learned the French language from Miss Tim. My new life began, and the suicidal thoughts disappeared from my head.

My first job at Maison Chance was to make greeting cards for Christmas and special occasions to be sent to Europe. I loved painting and I am good at it. I promised myself that I would never give up painting.

In 2003 I went to Lyon with Nhi, another orphan from Maison Chance. It was my first time flying in a plane and I was full of different feelings. After a half hour sitting in the plane, an air hostess brought us the meal trays. I immediately refused, thinking that the air ticket was expensive as it was and now we had to spend more money on food? Miss Tim laughed, explaining to us that the meals were included in the air ticket!

In Lyon, we stayed at a Vietnamese benefactor's home while he was away. This home was in the district of Villeurbanne.

We came to Lyon to learn more about painting at a textile company where we were trained for three months. Taking the bus was a new practical experience for me. The first day Tim took us to the factory on the bus and she clearly explained to us how to recognize our stops. She stayed with us all morning, but she had to leave at lunch to do other business. So, we had to get the bus by ourselves on the way home. We were completely lost; we did not remember the bus number and by the end we tried six different buses trying to get home!

We were not familiar with the shopping hours here. In Vietnam we can shop at all hours anywhere in small shops or street stalls. But here in France it is difficult to find any food, and everything was more expensive. So, when Tim suggested to us that we buy cakes and pizzas, we immediately declined. We preferred to shop for food at the Asian groceries and to cook our own meals at home, so we could save some money.

We also went to Chamonix ourselves to look at the mountains with snow. We loved to play in the snow and this was the first time ever we saw the snow. Nhi and I tried to make marbles out of snow and when we ran into any trouble, people came to our rescue.

Three months passed quickly, and it was time to return to Vietnam with our new experience and knowledge from the training session in France.

Sixteen years after the accident, my son came to visit me. He was studying in Saigon, so he came quite regularly. After the graduation, he returned to Hue as a musician and we kept in contact. Sadly, my son turned out to be not a very good person. Maybe due to my absence, he did not have the guidance of a father while growing up.

Today, I am still working at the painting room at the Take Wing Center. I returned to my home and my new wife at Village Chance, a place designed for wheelchairs access.

I also use my spare time to play basketball at the Village courtyard. Here, I no longer feel sad or depressed. I am surrounded by friends with similar life circumstances.

# Vo Thi Thu Hien

*"Before coming to Maison Chance, I could not imagine any man would marry a girl like me. So, I gave up the marriage idea and made up my mind to be single for the rest of my life. But at Maison Chance I realized that everything is possible."*

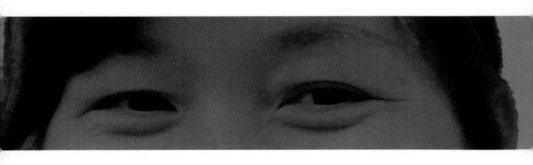

My name is Hien and I was born in 1983 in Vung Tau, about 40 miles southeast of Saigon. I have two elder brothers and an older sister. I did not know my father at all; he died when I was very little. My mother and brothers worked very hard in the fields to keep us alive. As for me I could not do anything. I was born disabled. I could stand up, but I could not walk very far. We did not know what was wrong with me. At that time people did not go to a hospital, they simply knew that I was not well.

I was born at home, not at a hospital since this was the common practice in the rural areas. When I turned ten, my mother was at the last stage of liver cirrhosis and she died of ascites, which is an abnormal buildup of fluid in the abdominal cavity. Her abdominal cavity swelled more and more until one day it erupted. The frightening image of that day was imprinted on my memory.

I lived with my siblings until I was 15 when they all got married and moved to separate houses. Life became so complicated for me then. I was dragged constantly from one household to the next. I could not help in any heavy work in the fields, just some light housework so my siblings made me feel that I was a burden to them all.

Finally, my elder brother took me to a French-sponsored hospital where the poor were admitted free of charge. My brother just left me there. In Vietnam the relatives of patients in a hospital had to feed and look after the patients themselves. Without any help, I had to look after myself.

After two months, the doctors advised me that they could not help me. I was diagnosed with progressive muscular dystrophy, a disease without any cure yet. They did not know what else they could do for me. But what could I do if I had to leave the hospital; I had nowhere to go and nobody to call on. I was frightened at the perspective of being homeless with no food to eat.

I pleaded with the doctors to let me stay a bit longer, so they agreed for me to be there for another week. By the end of that week I contacted my brothers and sister asking them to help me. But they told me 'that if I could get myself out then get out, otherwise...' It was obvious to me then that my siblings were no longer interested in helping me; they all knew that I could not get home by myself.

By then I did not wish to depend on my brothers and sister, knowing that I could not help them in any way. After that, I never heard from them again.

When my siblings abandoned me, my whole world collapsed. I was not allowed to stay on at the hospital, but I had nowhere to go, so I slept on the floor under the patients' beds. I hid myself in the toilet three or four times a day when the doctors made their rounds. I managed to survive like that for two weeks.

There was a kind visitor to the hospital, he brought food to patients and sometimes helped poor patients financially. He helped me by arranging a job of clearing tables at a coffee shop on Hoang Viet Street in Tan Binh District. The lady owner thought I was not disabled because I could stand up, so she agreed to give me the job. The coffee shop was on the ground floor of a three-story house. I slept on the second floor and all the facilities and work were on the ground floor. It was a great effort for me to deal with going up and down the stairs.

I must have been working there for two or three months, I cannot recall exactly, when the kind man came back to check to see how I was coping. He realized that not only the stairs were my problem but the owners lack of a caring attitude as well. So, he took me to an orphanage run by the French religious sisters. Here they accepted and trained orphans only since they had no facilities for the disabled, but in the end, they let me stay. They considered me also an orphan. They taught me to sew and I looked after the young ones and helped the sisters in other small jobs. After a year they asked me to find a more suitable place for my condition. The sisters knew Miss Tim and so I was accepted into Maison Chance in 1998.

The first few days I was at Maison Chance were not so easy since most of the residents were male and I was one of the few females. I felt isolated and lonely and I often cried.

I had not met any foreigners before, and so this young foreign lady really aroused my curiosity. At the beginning I was a bit timid with her, but she turned out to be kind and caring person and soon she became my second mother. I went to school and, as well as learning the French language, I kept on sewing. I did try to learn information technology but finally decided that sewing was still the most suitable for me. My present job is to look after guest reception and the products display/ sales room of Maison Chance.

Before coming to Maison Chance, I could not imagine any man would marry a girl like me. So, I gave up the marriage idea and made up my mind to be single for the rest of my life. But at Maison Chance I realized that everything is possible. I met a man, a male nurse in the Physiotherapy Center there, and we got married in 2004.

After the marriage we rented a room near Maison Chance, but this accommodation was not suitable for us at all. Not only did it have stairs, but the ground floor flooded during the rainy season. Luckily, when the apartments at Village Chance were completed we moved in and have lived there ever since.

We now have two beautiful daughters, Hien Vy is ten and Hien Mai only three and a half. The second pregnancy was so painful that I could no longer stand up. I had to use the wheelchair from then on.

I do not have any regrets about my old family. My nieces and nephews came looking for us when they studied in Saigon. I keep in touch with them occasionally since I wished my children to know their roots, but we no longer felt close.

I am happy here at Village Chance with my family. I have begun my new leaf of my book of life. I believe that life often is challenging but we have to face it and overcome it. Life is beautiful with all the presents that life has given me. Thank you, Mother Tim, for all the precious gifts.

# Dinh Cong Duy

*"My mother kept repeatedly asking me, 'Would you like to leave or to stay?' And each time my firm answer to her was, 'I'll leave'. I wish to start a new life at Maison Chance".*

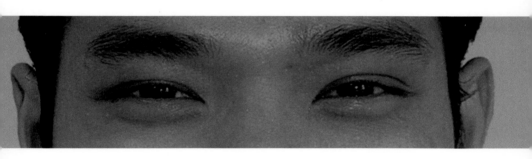

Every person born has a personal name.

According to Vietnamese tradition, a personal name is not only used to address a person, but it also carries a meaning expressing the wishful thoughts of our parents and grandparents for the best future of their offspring.

My name is Cong Duy. I was the first-born child of my parents and the source of joy and hope for them as a young couple then. So, my name Duy could mean "thinking or thoughts" and it could also mean "uniqueness", and the word "cong" chosen by my grandmother means "successes". Therefore, Cong Duy is the name symbolizing "intellectual successes".

I was born normal like many other children, but when I was five, I contracted a severe disease that changed my life completely. I could never be normal like other children again.

How did I become sick and why?

It happened one afternoon after I came back from my maternal grandparents. I was well; I ate, played and did all my chores as normal. When I became feverish, my parents thought it was just a normal childhood fever like all the other children they knew. However, I felt hotter and hotter and finally my temperature reached over 104 degrees Fahrenheit as shown on the thermometer. My parents became panicky and they hastily took me to the hospital.

At that time the 12-plus mile trip from home to the hospital was not an easy task. My father and his old bicycle struggled slowly on the slippery muddy dirt road, with my mother and me in her arms on the back seat. When we finally reached the hospital, I was admitted directly to the emergency room. The doctor on duty confirmed that I was having a very high temperature, but he could not tell us what the cause was.

My fever kept on raging for days on end. I slipped into a coma and was put on total life support with an oxygen tank and intravenous feeding. After a week, my condition did not improve and even worsened, so the doctor took my father aside and advised him that he take me home. The hospital could not give any further help and it was better for me to die at home than to die in the hospital. My father was very shocked at these words, but he courageously pleaded with the doctor to give me an injection of Teneurin as the last resort. If I did not come out of the coma then he would take me home.

The medication Teneurin, a French product, is a transmembrane protein used in severe case like mine and it was frightfully expensive.

The cost of one injection was as much as two grams of gold and that was a lot of money. My father did not care how much it cost as long as it could save me.

After the injection I slowly came out of the coma. As for me, I was indeed resurrected by that injection. However, I noticed that I no longer could use my arms. My grandmother had to feed me as she lovingly comforted me, "Eat, my child. You have to eat to get well quickly." Every member of my extended family came to visit me with gifts and treats to celebrate my miraculous recovery. But still I could not lift my arms up to receive a piece of orange from my grandmother's hand. She had to place it in my mouth for me. After a few days I was not better, and I went through another specialist's test. The result showed that my paralysis was due to the complications of poliomyelitis.

I was discharged after a month of treatment in the hospital. My father refused to accept the fact that his normal healthy boy is now a cripple. He had discussions with my mother and decided to leave Quang Ngai with my uncle to take me back to Ho Chi Minh City for further treatment.

We arrived at the Children's Hospital One where I was admitted, but the doctors took one look at me and shook their heads. They could not help me. The critical time for rehabilitation was lost; I was kept too long at the provincial hospital. My father nevertheless pleaded with the doctors to allow me to stay on at the hospital, so I had a chance of further treatment. After three months at the hospital, my father had run out of all the cash. There was nothing much he could do, so he and my uncle decided to take me home.

My father related this story later that on the way back from the bus station neither my father nor my uncle had any money to pay the motorbike taxi rider, but the driver kindly accepted a cucumber and a bundle of water spinach from our garden for the fare.

From then on, my body was as weak and pliable as a string of rice noodles. I stayed in the same position where I was placed, and I had no control of my body. However, my father thought "where there's life there's hope", so he searched everywhere for well-respected traditional doctors. He went from one village to the next searching and he spent all his money, but I did not make any improvement. By the end he had to resign himself to give up any hope and to accept what fate dealt to me.

As you can imagine, for a young newly wedded couple in a poor countryside, the task of providing all the necessities to care for a handicapped child was not easy. My parents often ran into financial difficulty and they even had to work harder when my next three siblings were born. My father and mother worked at any jobs, no matter how hard, as long as it brought in some cash.

My next younger sister took care of all the household chores as well as taking care of her two younger siblings and her elder paralyzed brother. She cooked for us and kept us clean; a hard job even for a grown up and yet she was still a child herself. But she managed to do all of these tasks.

During that hard time, we could not afford to have a TV at home, so at night we all went over to the neighbor's home to watch theirs and of course it was my sister who carried me over on her back.

I looked forward to special festivals and celebratory occasions because my parents would be at home to take us out visiting. The best time was Tet, our Lunar New Year, because no matter what, my parents would come back to celebrate Tet with the family. On the afternoon of New Year's Eve, they would line us up to have our annual ritual cleansing bath to welcome the New Year.

As I grew up I realized that I would never have a normal life like the others and every time when I saw kids of my age playing I felt bitter about my fate. I lived with an inferiority complex, withdrawing into my own self like a snail. The depression followed me day and night. I felt suicidal and one day, when my parents were away, I did try to bite my tongue to kill myself. But death did not want to take me. My sister found me, and she ran for help. I was saved.

After five years of immobility, I slowly learned to pull myself up and drag myself along the windowsill. And slowly I learned to sit up on my own and to feed myself, even with much difficulty. As time went by, my health improved, I even tried to move myself around with the help of two plastic chairs. I felt happy and encouraged, and my limited mobility helped me to communicate with the outside world. During the day my parents were at work and my siblings were at school, so I was left at home on my own.

Since the 1990s, drought, flood and insect plagues destroyed the crops in our region. To make a living, my father and his friend had to travel to Saigon and even further places for work, so my poor mother and my younger siblings had to take care of all the family chores as well as the hard work in the fields. Transportation costs were prohibitive, so my father only came home once a year at Tet, our Lunar New Year. When in Saigon, my father continued searching for a place where I could be professionally cared for. He believed that was the only way I could be treated, taught and trained so that I could survive independently when they could no longer look after me. After many years of searching in Saigon, my father heard from a distant uncle that there was a home of compassion called "Maison Chance."

My father was excited and asked the uncle to give him an introduction to this home. The distant uncle also emphasized, "She is my friend." Hearing this, my father was full of hope. He wrote to tell my mother and me. After a year, the uncle informed my parents that everything was arranged, and they should bring me to Saigon.

I still remember that was in 1999, around October in the Lunar

Calendar. It started getting cold where we were with the winter rain and the bitter winds. My parents had discussions with their parents and other members of the extended family and everyone agreed that I should go. They believed "That's the only way Duy can improve his health, have an education, and live among others in the outside world. If we keep Duy at home, he would remain a useless handicapped person all his life, a burden to his family and his community."

We knew that my leaving home was a blessing, but still at that time my mother strongly opposed to my leaving. She argued that with my frail health and without any close family to care for me I would suffer. We convinced her by the end with one condition; that was that she would accompany me to Saigon, so she could see my new life with her own eyes.

We left home one morning in the pouring rain; after a day and a night on an overcrowded bus crawling along the 530 miles of bumpy road, we arrived at my aunt's house in Saigon. The atmosphere in that house was depressing, it seemed to fill up with tears from my aunt and my mother, who repeatedly asked me this same question, "Do you want to go or to stay?" and each time, I answered definitely, "I want to go." I wanted to start a new life at Maison Chance.

Late one Tuesday afternoon, a Vespa stopped in front of my aunt's house, and two men came in to visit. One of the two men was the distant uncle, the other was Mr. Vu. Both claimed to be friends of Miss Tim, founder of Maison Chance. During the conversation the distant uncle told my father: "Vu and I have had everything arranged, however there is one small problem. We need a sum of five million dong (US $132) for a feast to thank the manager and the concierge of Maison Chance."

Hearing this, my father thought carefully and enquired, "So when do you need this money?" Immediately, the uncle said: "The sooner the better!"

After this conversation, my parents had to ask my aunt if they could borrow five million dong (about 220US dollars) from her. Of course, she only had two million dong (about 88 US dollars). My father went to all his friends and acquaintances to borrow the rest.

Four days later the uncle turned up with his friend on his Vespa. They came to pick me up, but before they left they told me to stick to the story that I was an orphan who sold lottery tickets in the streets and that I had met the uncle, but I did not know him. And they informed my parents that they could not follow us, and they were not allowed to visit me. I was an orphan without any close relatives!

My parents cried hearing this but for my future they kept quiet and accepted the story. My father paid them the five million. Later I found out that the entire story was a lie; the money was not for the expenses as they claimed because at that time there was neither concierge nor manager at Maison Chance. There was only Mother Tim and other teachers.

When we arrived at Maison Chance, I was taken to the office where two men and a woman foreigner were talking. Later I found out the foreigner was Mother Tim. They sat me in a lounge chair, I bowed my head to greet them and the interview began. The uncle told Mother Tim that they found me crawling in the streets selling lottery tickets.

Listening careful to the story, Mother Tim turned to me to enquire about my family circumstances. Of course, I could not be truthful; I was bound by the agreement. I therefore told Tim my story invented by these two men, so I could be admitted to Maison Chance.

When Mother Tim decided to accept me, I was half happy and half frightened.

I was happy knowing I would have a place to live, a place to study and a place where I could have physiotherapy treatment and all the other miraculous things that were unknown to me.

I was frightened thinking about the lie. What would happen if Mother Tim found out. Would she throw me out? What would happen if I missed my family? Am I allowed to telephone them or to go to visit them? These questions were like dark clouds in my head.

Lanh was my personal helper when I was first admitted to Maison Chance. He assisted me in my daily living, my personal hygiene, my clothes, my food and even my sleep. Due to lack of beds, at the beginning I had to share a bed with another member. Sometimes I slept in the physiotherapy room, right next to a vacant block of land overgrown with weeds and at night the sounds of different insects combined with the sound of the wind among the leaves to create a scary atmosphere which frightened me.

I began my new life without any excitement. I did not have a wheelchair, so I was unable to go anywhere. It was not much different from when I was in the countryside. The following few days I tried to move around with the help of two plastic chairs again. When Mother Tim saw me trying to be mobile, she bought me a small wheelchair. I was very small at 14 years old. When I got my 'legs' to move around I started participating in the communal life with other members at Maison Chance.

In the morning, I went to have my physiotherapeutic treatment, and, in the afternoon, I attended different classes conducted at Maison Chance. Here I learned reading and writing. I also noticed that at leisure time, some of the residents enjoyed playing computer games expertly, so I asked to join the information technology class hoping that one day I could be just as skillful at computer games and I also could be an expert in on-line football like the others.

Another special feature at Maison Chance was the frequent visits by foreigners. Some members of Maison Chance could welcome and communicate with them in their own languages and this inspired me to have another dream, "When can I communicate with the foreign visitors?" I applied to attend the French language class run by Mother Tim. I was doing three different classes simultaneously; I went to Vietnamese school for general education, I was being trained in computer science and I was learning a foreign language. In 2004 I graduated from high school with my High School Certificate and this occasion pleased me immensely. After so many years of hard work, my dream was realized.

But did you realize that to achieve all this, my family and I had to lie that I was an orphan without any family support. My parents suffered a great deal for this lie, not only because they had to abstain from visiting, talking and writing to me but also, they had to listen to people's criticism that they just got rid of me to avoid any burden. They felt as if a knife cut through their hearts when hearing these cruel critics, so my mother decided to leave home and go to Saigon selling lottery tickets, hoping they would run into me sometimes.

And we did nearly every day. We secretly met at a coffee shop. When my paternal grandma came to visit me despite her age and the distance, but she stayed for only two weeks. I could only secretly see her as I did with my mother. So, I decided to tell Mother Tim the truth about my family. Mother Tim understood, and she forgave me.

By the end I managed to return to my village for a visit after four long years of separation. My parents and my siblings were very happy seeing me again and the whole village came to see me. And I proved to them that I left home not to save my parents the burden but to improve my future life.

In 2006, I was lucky. I was invited to visit Europe and Mother Tim gave me permission to go and also helped me preparing for my travel. Besides sight-seeing while in Europe, I had to assist Mother Tim in introducing the audience to the activities of Maison Chance at four fund raising events in France, Switzerland and Belgium. During the three months in Europe, I learned a great deal in cultural understanding, in social interaction and especially in my French language.

When I returned to Saigon around the middle of 2007, I began my job at Maison Chance. I was responsible for the internet and later, in 2009, I became the web master. I was not very confident in my work at the beginning but later, with the help of volunteers as well as other experts in the office, I slowly gained some confidence in my work.

When I was attending classes at Maison Chance I met Thuy, who was also a member of Maison Chance. Thuy came to live here a few years after me to be rehabilitated after a bad accident and trained for her future. We fell in love and we understood and respected each other. Together we built our future. On the April 4, 2011 we celebrated our marriage. We like to share our lives in happiness and in sadness, in rich and in poor.

At the end of 2009 Thuy was successful in an entrance exam of an international company and she works in District One. I am manager of the Project Office of Maison Chance. We both have jobs, so we moved into an apartment at Village Chance where members of Maison Chance can have permanent suitable accommodations for handicapped persons like me.

I am happy with my dear wife in our apartment. Thuy loves and cares for me.

I often wonder for those who were unlucky like me, if there was no Maison Chance, where would we be? What would become of us? How would we survive? These questions are carved in my memory with my heartfelt thanks to Mother Tim who has sacrificed her youth to bring happiness and faith in humanity for the less fortunate like me.

Thank you!

# Tran Tat Cuong

*"The most meaningful time of my life were the months, the years living at Maison Chance. This was my true family and it was not at Thanh Hoa, but it was at Binh Hung Hoa with Mother Tim and all my siblings, uncles and aunties at Maison Chance."*

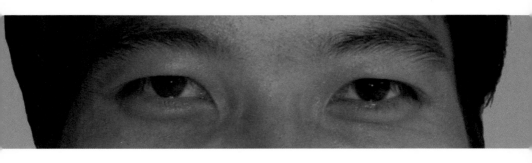

My name is Tran Tat Cuong. I was born at a small village in Thanh Hoa Province in the north of Vietnam. I left there quite a long time ago; over fifteen years now. I have a vague memory of my childhood. I had an old and sick mother and some siblings, but I hardly knew them. As for my father, I don't even know who he is. We all lived in a run-down bamboo hut on the beach that was regularly blown away in every windy storm.

I was often away from home. I was a beggar like most of the other villagers, but I was so poor that I did not have any choice. I was fatherless, so no one took me fishing in my village. But all fishing was done by men only; therefore I ended up being a street kid selling chewing gum for my living. And to earn my living I had to venture further away from home, so I followed one of my older buddies in these adventures. First, we went to Hanoi, then down to Hue, and sometimes even as far as Saigon.

I remembered clearly a furious stormy night in Saigon when I was eight years old. It rained, and the wind howled for three days non-stop. I could not sell any gum and I had not a single penny in my pocket. This angered my older companion and he beat me up so badly that I had to escape from him and I have not seen him since.

By now I was a professional street kid and I lived and worked on the streets. I slept on any pavement to pass the night. I shared my life with other street kids of similar circumstances as me for over two months, then I met another street kid and we became friends. We lived together for over two years sharing all we had to survive.

One evening like any other evening, we were begging at the Bay Hien Cross roads when we saw a young foreigner on motor bike stopping near us. We were so excited hoping that she would give us a lot of money. However, she introduced herself to us; her name was Tim. We talked together for a while, and she asked us if we would like to live with a family who would take care of us. We immediately accepted her offer. She then took us to have a bowl of beef balls. She did not take us home then but promised to come and meet us the next day.

At first, I was not used to the strict rules and regulations applied at Maison Chance. To tell the truth, I did not feel comfortable at all surrounded by strangers, especially those in the wheelchairs. I was frightened by their disability. I had never seen so many people in wheelchairs in one place like this. However, as time went by, I realized that the people in wheelchairs were not much different; they were just unable to walk about. There were also other kids like me and not long afterwards we became siblings.

When I first arrived at Maison Chance I was illiterate, but like all members of Maison Chance I was sent to school to be educated. I was a good student and I was often the best in my classes. I studied both French and English languages. But due to my laziness, I gave up my studies, ignoring the encouragement of Mother Tim. I was more interested in making a lot of money. Finally, I took up Mother Tim's advice. I resumed my studies in computer science and came back to teach other children at Maison Chance. Mother Tim accepted me back so many times and she readily forgave me for my stupidity and frivolity.

In 2011, Mother Tim suggested that I should try to contact my birth family. I was then 24 and since I had not made any contact with my family for a long time, it was a difficult task. I believed that my birth mother was long dead, but I did not find any evidence to confirm this. In the end, I found out that they had always lived in the same spot and I decided to go for a visit.

A few days before the journey I received the news that my birth mother had been dead for the last three years. She died of alcoholism and madness. I was very sad hearing this, but I decided to go back to find out who I really was. My small village in Thanh Hoa Province remained unchanged, there were still beggars and poverty could be seen everywhere.

I found an elder sister and two younger brothers. I had been trying to maintain some kind of family relationship, but with much difficulty. We had nothing in common and I felt that a biological link does not mean very much to me any longer.

The most meaningful time of my life were the months and the years living at Maison Chance. This was my true family and it was not at Thanh Hoa, but it was at Binh Hung Hoa with Mother Tim and all my siblings, uncles and aunties at Maison Chance.

# Nguyen Ba Bong

*"'I am in pain therefore I am still alive,' a voice floating by my ears... someone cried out loud... The big crane lift... the fast speed boat... the blurred images of one then two doctors... These were my vague memories of that moment of being half awake and half unconscious. Eight years have passed and yet these images and noises follow me like a nightmare. Maybe they will follow me for the rest of my life."*

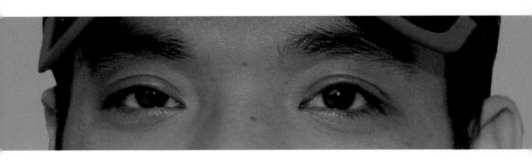

I am Nguyen Ba Bong, 25 years old. I was born in the small village of Nam Son in Hai Duong Province in North Vietnam. It is a traditional agricultural village and we worked mainly in the fields or in the orchards or gardens. However, fast industrial development slowly took over the agricultural land, filling it with factories and industrial zones.

Such fast development for a third world country was a good thing, but it also brought along some bad side effects. The most obvious effect could be seen at the village level since the young villagers were no longer interested in working in the fields. Also, no more land was left for growing food crops. Everybody liked to leave for the big cities for work, and I am not an exception either.

When I was 17, I was excited about moving to Ho Chi Minh City to begin my new life. This was where I placed all my hopes for a better future and this was also the place where I lost it all. I was no longer my complete self.

At Ho Chi Minh City, I found a job working with a few of my friends from the same village. Our job was to hook the cables to the containers, so they could be lifted onto the waiting ships. These ships came from all different countries and would move the goods worldwide. Our work flow depended on the movement of the shipping companies, no matter what time of the day or night. It was hard work, but I was happy to earn enough money to keep myself and sometimes I could save some to send to my family.

Once when we were on night duty, my job was to hook the cables to the containers on the ship deck, so they could be lifted to the ship's hull. It was late, and we were all tired, but still there was a lot to be done. Suddenly I lost my balance and fell from the deck into the hull. I could have fallen from more than 10 meters (over 30 feet) high. The long fall knocked me out, but I could vaguely remember that moment with some undistinguished noises and images in my mind; the moment that changed my life completely.

A few days later I woke up in a white hospital room and I was told that I had damaged my neck bone. I was optimistic thinking that it was simple work accident and that I would recover after some treatment. However, I was wrong. In the hospital, I was put through so many tests and treatment. For fifteen days I suffered different tortures trying to release my fused spinal cord and I had to go through an operation to rebuild my spinal cord. This was followed by days of post operation treatment. I had to take so many pills daily.

After two months, I was still bedridden. I had no sensation in my hands or my feet. My neck was still locked immobile in the neck trap. I still hoped that everything would come back and that it was a question of time so that I needed to be patient.

One morning, when the doctors did their rounds, I noticed that my elder brother was called over to exchange some information. My brother turned his head to look at me and tears rolled down his cheek. I did not know why but seeing his tears I felt uneasy. I asked him why the tears, but he refused to answer my question. I felt frightened of what may happen to me.

Do you know that even though no one mentioned anything about it, I felt the gravity of my condition? I saw patients being discharged even though there was no change in their health and their relatives wondered if their loved ones would ever recover and when they would recover. One day I gathered all my courage and asked the doctor, "When would I be well again and when can I leave?"

He answered, "Maybe three to six months but you need to keep doing your exercises and eat well so you don't have atrophied muscles." I felt calm and assured hearing that it may take six months for me to recover.

After three months, I was transferred to the rehabilitation hospital in District Eight. There, I had to do all sorts of exercises to regain simple, everyday life movements such as how to hold things and how to move my body to one side. All these movements were natural to everyone, but it was a big effort for me. For example, brushing my teeth; I spent one-week practicing brushing my teeth to no avail. This drove me to tears and rage. I argued with others for no reason at all. At times I felt hopeless, but I kept up with my exercises, clinging to the hope that I may recover.

However, I suddenly realized that if I stayed on this hospital bed I would never recover, and I knew now that I would never walk with my legs again. A cruel reality, now I understood why my brother was full of tears, why the relatives asked such questions, and why there were long-term patients who did not make any improvement even after years of treatment. My observation and my research provided me with an answer; once the spinal column was damaged, it was difficult for the spinal cord to recover and most of the time it never recovered.

I fell into a deep depression and I neglected my exercises and my food. I could not believe that I would never walk again. What would be the rest of my life? How would my friends treat me? Would they feel pity for me? Would my whole life be attached to a wheelchair?

But that was my reality and I could not shake free of it. My tears rolled down uncontrollably, and I kept crying. I cried for my fate; I was young. I was only 18 years old. I would have a long life and there were so many new things to be discovered and waiting for me. It was painful to watch as my muscles slowly atrophied and my ability to help myself deteriorated. I could not even feed myself.

Then the six months passed, and I was still the same. No improvement. I was obsessed with negative thoughts. Maybe death would be the only escape from being a burden to myself and to my family?

Luckily a change arrived unexpectedly. It was not a magic change that I had been praying for. It was Maison Chance that offered to help me both physically and spiritually. This experience changed my negative thinking about life and I realized the real value of humanity. Before I went to Maison Chance, I heard about this charity founded by a young Swiss lady named Tim who offered total care, education and training to the disabled and the orphans.

Due to my disadvantaged family condition, I was accepted into Maison Chance. Here I met other people with disabilities like mine;

some were born with them and some were the results of the poison chemical Agent Orange. There were also orphans and street kids.

Although everyone suffered a different misfortune, they all showed their positivity and humanity. I myself received so much love and sharing from everyone from Mother Tim to the youngest members of the House and this changed my attitude toward my own disability. I often asked myself how they could be happy when they have similar problem like me? I asked myself why I was always pessimistic and felt an inferiority complex? Suddenly it dawned on me that the real value of life was so simple; it was the sharing, the mutual love and support given to people, and the help given them to stand against all life challenges.

One strong impression I had of Maison Chance was my first encounter with a young man about 20 years old. He was also member of the House. He had a funny walk as if he was drunk. I asked myself how he could possibly be drunk at this early hour of the day. A few minutes later he fell over and it took him a long time to get up. Then he went into his room. The next day I learned his name was Linh and that he had suffered brain damage since he was a child, so he found it difficult to move around. I felt ashamed learning about Linh and I regretted having such bad thoughts about people.

My new life started with all good intentions. I left behind my pessimistic thoughts and my negative life. It suited my physical health to apply to study computer science at the Take Wing Center. After two years studying hard, I improved a lot, in part thanks to the support of my teachers and my friends. From knowing little about computers, I became skillful in using computers. So, I got a job and even though it paid moderately, it affirmed my ability to still work. I am not a useless person. I had to try much harder to prove that disabled people like us could still work and we could conquer our unlucky fate.

However, knowing people's attitudes towards the disabled like us, I was still troubled by an inferiority complex. Sometimes I felt like crying when I tried to stop the bus and it kept on going. Sometimes I was refused service at restaurants because they did not want a disabled person to bring bad luck to their establishment; it was an old superstition. Going to the toilets was another problem; at public places, like hospitals; schools, and bus stations, there were no toilets for the handicapped.

I started to devise projects commensurate with my health. For two years, I studied computer science at the Take Wing Center. I worked hard, enthusiastically spurred on by my friends' support and my professor's patience. At first, I knew nothing about computers, but now I can acquit myself pretty well with computers and I have a stable job. My salary is modest, but what is most important is that I can work. I am not a useless man. And I want to prove that the handicapped are still capable of fulfilling our own needs.

At Maison Chance, all was intended to facilitate the lives of the handicapped. However, in the rest of society, there is still plenty to do. Most Vietnamese don't know how to behave around us and towards us. I almost cried out in rage when we were victims of discriminatory behavior; for example, when the bus driver refused to pick us up along with our wheelchairs or when a restaurant simply refused to make room for us.

We also have difficulties in public places where there are stairs or doorsteps to cross. These obstacles are prevalent at hospitals, schools, cinemas, even toilets. We always depend on the help of those who carried us or push our wheelchairs. These obstacles never ceased to remind us of our conditions and they feed our inferiority complex.

Among my memories of Maison Chance, the most remarkable is one of Christmas celebrations. As I came from a Buddhist milieu, I knew nothing of Christmas. At Maison Chance, Christmas is not just a religious holiday. It is most of all the moment when everyone can meet everyone else.

We built a manger with historical Christmas characters, we decorated a Christmas tree, and everyone received a gift. I was filled with joy that first Christmas. I received a gift from the hands of Mother Tim. She had given me a shirt.

Here, I found equilibrium. I love life, now more than ever. And I rejoice as to what the future would bring. The wonderful world has many things waiting for me and I hope that the world will be free of wars, poverty, and natural catastrophes. And there will be no more babies born with disabilities and deformities.

Thank you everyone. Thank you, Mother Tim, for giving me a meaningful life.

# Nguyen Van Lam

*"I could let go but I could not be defeated. I would do my best to face any future challenges. I no longer have the use of my limbs, but I still have my heart and my brain. I could not possibly be a useless person."*

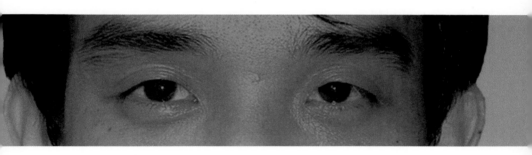

I am Lam. I was born in 1985 in Thanh Hoa, a poor province in the north central delta of Vietnam. My parents, who have four children, were peasants tilling the land for their living. Their life is closely attached to the buffalo and the plough.

When I graduated from high school, I was young and full of hope and expectation for a bright future. I asked permission from my parents to travel to the south to sit for a university entrance examination. My objective was to be on the inside of the gate of the University of Pedagogy where I would get the proper key to my future. On my departure, my younger siblings were full of tears; this would be the first time we lived apart. Seeing them cry I was so sad that I wanted to cry too but I had to tell myself to be brave since I was now a grown up. I had to be an example for my younger siblings.

Ho Chi Minh City was a busy and noisy with heavy traffic and luxurious high-rise buildings; a city of richness and prosperity, completely different from the poor, quiet county town where I grew up. It took a few days for me to adjust to the new life style. The first thing for me to do in this modern city was to find a job before even thinking about my long-term future plan.

For the first few months I tried all sort of works, from laboring to waiting on tables. I even went as far as Binh Phuoc to work the land. But all my hard work paid off, I received the letter informing me that I was admitted to the University of Pedagogy at Binh Phuoc. I let my parents know the good news immediately. I was overjoyed with my faith in my bright future. Everyone in my family was happy for me.

But my innocent happy student life and my bright future was interrupted by an event; a brief event of a few minutes and yet it changed my life completely and permanently.

I remembered that night at about 10 p.m.; I was riding my bike on the way to pick up one of my visiting relatives. The road was pitch-dark. Suddenly a pair of bright headlights blinded my vision. I tried to move to the side, but I was hit, and the bike and I were thrown over the side of the road. I laid immobile on the deserted dark road listening to my breath getting weaker and weaker. Once I heard a car driving past but my voice was not loud enough to be heard, and anyway people tend to drive fast at night on deserted roads.

I was in coma for a couple of days after the accident. When I woke up in Cho Ray hospital my whole body was immobile. After a medical examination and tests, I was diagnosed with fracture of the cervical cord and quadriplegia. To save me, they had to use many different treatments and surgery as well. I was tormented by the pain for days and I could not sleep nor eat, but the doctors did not dare to give me any pain killers or sleeping pills in case I relapsed into a coma again.

After a week of excruciating pain, I went through a twelve-hour operation to reset my cervical cord. When I woke up I could hear voices and I could see everything around me, but my limbs were not movable. My paralyzed life depressed me so much that sometimes I wished for a peaceful ending. But when I thought of my parents, my siblings and the effort that I had put into my study, I could not give up. I still carried a strong hope that I would recover soon. I spent 45 days in the emergency room. I was fed intravenously, and an oxygen tank helped me to breathe.

I did not make any improvement in spite of all the treatments and medication. I knew that we were very poor, and my parents had to borrow money from everyone to cover my care. My family suffered a lot because of me. I felt so unhappy when I saw worry in my parents' face. I also felt sorry for my younger brother since he had to give up his school to look after me in the hospital. My girlfriend rushed in to see me in tears when she heard of my accident, and she took two weeks off from the university to care for me. She supported me through the painful moments and all I could do was to lie there immovable.

We lost all hope when the doctor informed us that my injury was very serious and maybe I may not recover. He went on to say that the family should brace themselves with the fact that I may not survive. It was a big shock for my family; they would not accept my possible death at such a young age. My father pleaded with the doctor to let me stay on for any possible treatment until the day I die.

Two weeks later, my health started improving, but the girl I loved had to go back to her normal life and study. She left in sadness and in tears. I knew we were both in pain, but I tried to struggle against it and to see her off with a smile.

The next day, the doctor decided to transfer me to the Saigon Rehabilitation Center in District Eight where I was given intensive physiotherapeutic treatment. Like a newborn baby I had to learn to sit up, to stand, to turn over, and to feed myself. Everything seemed to be strange and new and everything seemed to be difficult to learn.

My parents had to return to the country to earn money to support my hospital care. My poor little brother Luong, who is very calm and quiet by nature, stayed on to look after me. He was very small and yet he took over the heavy duty of taking care of his disabled brother. Knowing that because of me he had to sacrifice his own studies, a guilt complex slowly poisoned me.

My parents also worried that my brother, who was just 16, would be able to carry the burden of looking after a handicapped brother. Would he be able to feed me, keep me clean and fulfill my other special needs? However, my brother did the job better than everyone expected. After he gave me breakfast, he took me to the physiotherapy room for exercises and after that he cleaned me up and fed me. Some nights my pain was so bad that I became feverish. My brother would stay up all night to keep me cool with a wet rag. He was exhausted and was found sleeping sitting next to my bed. Really what he did for me could only be performed by a parent to their own child.

So, my life came to a halt. All my dreams, my expectations, my wishes for a bright future suddenly evaporated into the floating clouds. Where was the young healthy man? Where was the innocent student? I would be a disabled person sitting in a wheelchair for life? Dark thoughts invaded my head and I heard a voice whispering in my ear, "It is better to die than to live as a handicapped person."

The bad news caused my family to collapse. My mother had no more tears to cry. And although everyone encouraged me to get over this shock, my despair grew inside me unchecked, pushing me in the corner of hopelessness. I avoided people and I was obsessed with the idea of death. I set myself apart from people, even friends and relatives. I was silent all day and in denial of my permanent disability. And I decided to cut off my love relationship knowing that I could not offer my love a happy life.

Those were truly the darkest days of my life, you know. I lived as if I was dead and I was desperately depressed. I lost my will to live and I was mentally in crisis. This was the big event; the shock of my life which I could not accept. I had witnessed so many similar cases and more than any others I understood very well their emotion, their psychological changes, and their thoughts. I knew them well, so I understood their behavior. But whenever I saw the sadness and the pain expressed on the faces of their loved ones, I could only think of my parents, my brother and my relatives and my friend who had been taken care of me. I could not betray them and cause them pain, and so my idea of suicide faded away in my head.

One beautiful spring day in December 2005 marked a change from the dark period of my life. As my brother pushed my chair around the hospital complex for relaxation, by chance we met Tim Aline, a gentle Swiss lady of about 30. She approached us smiling and she spoke to us in fluent Vietnamese enquiring about my circumstance. After listening to my story, she asked me, "So what is your dream now?" I answered straight away, "My dream is to get well again and to continue with my studies." Upon hearing my answer, she said, "Then I will help you." She then told me about Maison Chance, an establishment she founded to take care of and to train orphans and street kids as well as people with disabilities. I felt relieved of all my worries when we parted. Tim promised that when I was discharged from the hospital, we could come to see her at Maison Chance.

When my father came to take me home, I told him about the

meeting with Miss Tim. He was very excited and happy about the news. I assured my father that it would be good for me to remain at the hospital until after Tet and when I was discharged we would go to Maison Chance. My father left feeling a bit sad but hoping that I would overcome my present difficulty and my future life would be better.

Nightly I stayed awake wondering about my future. Could I do anything when I was still not strong enough with my useless limbs? I would have to depend on others for everything. I could let go but I could not be defeated. I would do my best to face any future challenges. I no longer had the use of my limbs, but I still had my heart and my brain. I could not possibly be a useless person. I regained my burning will to get on with my life and I would never think of killing myself again. I had to live to realize all my lifelong dreams until my last breath.

I had made up my mind to go on, but I could not foretell the future. The only certain thing was that my life was going to turn a new page. I might have to face many obstacles and pain on my new life road, but I believed that I would be able to overcome them. I knew for certain that, hidden behind all the pain, the sorrows and the difficulties, I would find a happy smile.

After I met Miss Tim, I felt much better mentally and spiritually. I was full of hope for a new bright future. On February 14, 2006, after my medical examination, the doctor decided that I was ready to be discharged. I was sent off by all the hospital staff, the patients and their relatives as if they were saying farewell a member of their own family. My brother and I were very moved by this. By now we only had the taxi fare to go to Miss Tim's house.

The taxi took forever to get to our destination. I was impatient to see my new home, but we got there finally. The taxi stopped in a crowded and noisy lane in front of Maison Chance. A young man on wheelchair came out to meet and greet us. He took us inside and introduced us to other members of the house.

Maison Chance was situated near Binh Hung Hoa Cemetery in a crowded outer suburb of Saigon. The neighborhood was inhabited by mainly working-class people who earned their living by manual labor, by driving trucks or by just selling lottery tickets. I was a bit scared to mix with them at the beginning but slowly I discovered that they were quite nice, and they had good relationships with Maison Chance.

After two months, my brother and I got used to the rhythm of life at Maison Chance. The illiterate members were sent to school to learn reading and writing while others attended training courses according to their own physical ability and aspirations.

During my first year at Maison Chance, my health was still not good. As a quadriplegic, and even though I did make some improvement with some of the muscles in my hands, I still could not hold on to anything. Still I persisted with my computer course. Twice a day I went to the physiotherapy room for exercise. It took me many hours to learn to feed myself and yet I still could not manage to do it well. I did feel depressed and defeated but each time I reminded myself that I had to persist in learning and with practice I should succeed in the end.

I went to my computer class after my physiotherapy and this was another test of my patience. The keyboard would not do what my fingers wished. It was very frustrating not being able to type the right word.

But I did prove to myself that nothing was impossible if I kept trying. And after two years of trying, I succeeded in using the keyboard. My physical health also improved, and I enrolled in English language class as well. At night I volunteered to teach the orphans at Maison Chance and other poor children from the neighborhood.

This made me happy even though it was the only a small useful thing that I managed to achieve so far.

Most of the children living at Maison Chance had been orphans or street kids; they had hardly experienced family protection or love. But since coming here, they were loved and cared for by Mother Tim and other members in the house. They all aspired to learn some profession. Some wished to become doctors, so they could look after the less fortunate, while others wished to become teachers, singers or actors. Since they came here they were much better off and happy, but I always noticed that somehow there was always a faraway look in their eyes.

I still remembered my inferiority complex when I first arrived here; it prevented me from communicating with others. But slowly I got used to the communal life style. I made friends with other members in the house. My first friends here were Hien, Tien Linh, Han and Duy. We all came from different backgrounds, but we all carried a sad past and we all tried to study for a better future of independent living.

As for me, I found a way of expressing my personal painful life experience through poetry. Whenever I felt sad, painful or happy, I expressed that feeling through poetic words. I wrote poems for myself, for my friends, for my country and for my family. I wrote to express the happiness and the painful breakup of love. I wrote about the social unfairness and I wrote about the sufferings of the less fortunate.

I secretly wished that one day my poems would be published so I could offer a small gift to the readers and to leave behind something of my own for the generations to come. And this wish was realized unexpectedly. The board of the Fund for Scholarship Pham Truong Tan decided to sponsor the publication of my first poetry collection under the title *"Why, My love."* It was launched publicly on August 3, 2011 at the Club House of DRD on Hoa Hung Street in District Ten.

I also had a CD of my poems produced and launched in November 2011. I was extremely happy and contented. All my impossible dreams were finally becoming a reality.

Today, I am married, and we live in a specially designed apartment suitable for wheelchair access at Village Chance. I teach computers and English to the children attending Village Chance primary school. I still dream and wish to work harder to overcome my own handicap and to realize many other dreams. I know I have to face many life challenges still, but I will not give up. I only live once, and I love my life. I love Maison Chance, my dearest second family; I love every one of them. It is Mother Tim who gave me my second life, my faith and my hope in humanity.

I will treasure every day I live, and I will make my life meaningful. Every day I welcome my happiness with a big smile and the wind will carry it to the horizon.

Once again, I would like to thank life, to thank my family, my friends and all others.

Thank you, Mother Tim, for having given me a meaningful life.

# Ngoc Han

*"The sensational feeling of being a father for the first time and holding my child in my withered arms left a permanent imprint in my memory for life."*

I am Ngoc Han. I was born a normal, cute chubby baby, but my future was cut short early due to a cruel illness I contracted when I was only four months old. And this changed my life drastically.

That day, I had a fever and my mother thought it was just the unavoidable childhood fever that all children experienced. However, my fever did not go away, and my temperature increased dangerously. My mother became worried, so she took me to the local hospital.

Vietnam just came out from a long, devastating war and the hospital was poorly equipped with minimum services. So, my mother had to wait until 9 p.m. before I was examined and by now my temperature was extremely high. To reduce it, the doctor soaked me in a bowl of cold water. But this did not do the trick; my temperature continued to rise. I started having serious convulsions, my limbs shook violently, and I foamed at my mouth. My mother was so frightened that she had to call my father home, and he was working far from home.

My father rushed back and seeing the hopeless situation at the local hospital, he decided to take me to Saigon, hoping to get better treatment for me there. There, I was examined by specialists and after my examination they said to my father, "You took your son in a bit late. Even though he had passed the most dangerous zone, the effects of the disease will be permanent. I am afraid he will never have a normal life like other kids."

Therefore, my childhood was associated mainly with the hard work of my parents caring for me during the long period of time I spent at home and at hospitals and rehabilitation centers. My parents spent an uncountable amount of money on my treatment, including acupuncture, but without much improvement. By the end, they had to accept that my disease was not curable; the aftereffects of the high fever left me with the total paralysis of both my legs and my right arm. My left arm was still functional. Later on, I learned that what I had was Japanese encephalitis.

As I grew up I started observing things happening around me and I started asking questions which pained the adults. I asked, "Why can the other kids run around playing? Why can they use their hands and I can't?"

However, I had to admit that I did have a happy childhood living with my family. I enjoyed being taken out on the bike every afternoon by my father. I loved being carried on the back of my elder sister as she ran around playing with friends and I prized how my grandmother tenderly taught me how to walk in the front of the house.

Those happy days unfortunately were ended with the fatal accident of my eldest brother whom my parents had hoped to be able to take over the family duty for them in their old age. At that time, I was still too young to understand; I always believed that my eldest brother had to go away for a long time, but he would be back. The family atmosphere was stressful with the sound of my mother crying from the bedroom and my father's long heavy sighs from the lounge room. As for me, I just sat on one spot staring into space, wondering.

By the end, to fill up the painful emptiness, my parents decided to have two more children. So, from being the youngest child of the family, I became the elder brother of two younger siblings. And I was no longer the priority in my family.

When I turned ten and I had thought a bit more about things, I asked my mother if I could go to school. She told me that I was still too little, but if I was a normal child I should have had at least year four or five of school by now. That year my next youngest brother was going to start year one as well.

Watching my sister and brother preparing for their new school year, I felt a pain in my heart; I felt sorry for myself. Other children of my age who went to school acquired so much knowledge, but for me I could not even read or write. At dinner time, listening to my sister and brother noisily telling my parents about their school work, I had to swallow my food hastily to get away from the table and hide myself in a corner, so they could not see the jealousy on my face.

My entire world was my TV and the window. Nothing was sadder than having no friend to talk to and no close siblings to share my thoughts with. I knew that my parents loved me, but I could not help feeling that I was a stranger among them all; a person being abandoned by his own family. The bigger my siblings became the sadder I became. I was permanently obsessed with the idea that today was the same as yesterday or the day before that.

Although I knew that not everyone was born under a lucky star and that I had a good happy life, I still asked myself, "Why can't I be like other normal people? Why am I destined to be one of the less fortunate minorities of the disabled?"

Then my luck changed after I saw a TV program on Maison Chance where they care for and train people like me, so they can work at jobs that I had thought impossible. I asked my parents to search for the address of this house, but when they learned of my intention to apply for a place at Maison Chance, they all tried to stop me. They said that I was at home among the family who helped me with everything. Why should I move to Maison Chance?

I disagreed with my family totally. They did not realize that I wished to live like other normal people. I longed to go to school and to have friends. It was important for me to be able to participate in a normal social life, so I would no longer be a burden for my family or society.

I was determined I would go to Maison Chance. On the journey, the 44 miles of dusty road and the hot Saigon sun tired me out. At Maison Chance everything and everyone were completely new and seemed so strange to me. A lady came to show me my room and greeted my parents. That's how I officially took up residence at Maison Chance.

At the beginning, it was a bit difficult for me since I had to look after myself mostly. My parents were not next to me to assist me and I had not made any friends here yet. Slowly, I got more use to the new rhythm of life and other members became friendlier and were much closer to me. Six years was not a long time in a whole life time but for me it was very significant because during that period of time I had changed my way of thinking completely. And I changed in many other things as well.

I remember when I first lived at Maison Change I thought everything was strange and I felt so lonely. I had to learn the alphabet and to read and write with the little children. Then I choose to be trained in computer science. Students in this course were mainly paraplegics in wheelchairs and the standard of knowledge we achieved was moderate, so even after three years training in computer science, we found getting a job was impossible.

For me, I thought of returning home several times, but then I thought, "Returning home? What for? Do I wish to come back to the beginning? Here at least I have friends; some would spend hours chatting with me over a cup of coffee sharing our joy and sorrows. I really should stay on and improve my skill, maybe one day..."

Fortunately, when we were in our darkest moment, lady luck came and smiled on us. In midyear 2010 we all got offers for suitable jobs with a website design company in Ho Chi Minh City. I still remember the exciting feeling when I got my first pay. It was not a big pay, but we were happy because it was the fruit of our own labor. We spent our first pay to have a feast at a restaurant near Maison Chance.

I now had a secure job, and, like everybody, I wished to have a family, so I could come home to a family meal prepared by a loving wife and to play with my children. This was just a dream, but life has some surprises. In 2011 I got to know a lady at Maison Chance who was disabled like me. We fell in love and after a few months, we got married in August 2012 at Village Chance. The wedding was a happy occasion with the participation of both our families, our relatives, our friends and all the members of Maison Chance.

Mother Tim had witnessed our love from the start to the happy end. She is like a messenger who brings hope and happiness to everyone at Maison Chance.

A few months later, my wife was with child. We were happily awaiting our first born who arrived on July 22, 2013. My daughter was welcomed into the world by the whole family. She was a beautiful little girl with skin as white as snow and she looked like me! The sensational feeling of being a father for the first time and holding my child in my withered arms left a permanent imprint in my memory for life.

On January 19, 2016 our son was born. I felt comforted and relaxed after work being among my family with my wife and kids.

In spite of my unlucky fate, life has taught me so many lessons. I have overcome so many obstacles and I love this life. But I realize there is more for me to treasure, and that treasure includes my friends who share my happiness and my sadness. I can look after myself, I have a job and I am not a useless person. And I am also happy to have my love that encourages and helps me to face all of life's challenges.

Thank you, Maison Chance. And thank you all my dear friends who taught me that no matter how difficult life can be, with love and hope I will succeed.

# Y Nam

"Mother Tim carried me on her back and took me to the top of the highest mountain on Phu Quoc Island to look at the view. She emphasized that life is beautiful, and no matter what we would keep on living. So now I have no intention to end my life."

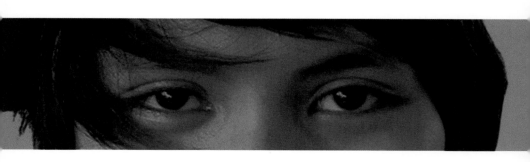

I am Y Nam. I am from the minority group Bana. I was born and grew up in Kontum, a province on the Western Central Highlands of Vietnam. I am the fourth child from a family of 11. I don't know much about all my siblings since I left home when I was nine.

I wished to go to school but my family was too poor to pay for my school fee; all the money was used up to pay for my elder siblings, so I missed out. I was sent to a local orphanage where they taught me to write and read. My parents came to visit me every few months, so I was not very close to them.

A few years later, when I was 13, I contracted myelitis, a fever that caused the inflammation of the spine. That happened a few days before Tet, the Vietnamese New Year. While waiting for my father to pick me up to go home to celebrate Tet with my family, I was not feeling very well. I was tired most of the time and I thought I had the flu. They took me to see a shaman, but it was useless. My fever was not abated and a week later I was paralyzed. I was immobile on the bed, but no one suspected that I would become disabled. When my father came to fetch me, I did not want to go to the hospital. I wanted to go home to be with the family for Tet. Two days later, my condition worsened. I could not even feed myself, so my family took me to the hospital where I was hooked on to a ventilator to help my breathing.

I was in the provincial hospital for two months and my parents wanted to transfer me to a hospital in Saigon where to treatment was superior, but it also meant it would cost much more. This was when some kind people helped us to pay the hospital bills.

So, I was admitted to the hospital. I lived in pain and fear for so many months. I was in the room with terminally ill people waiting to die. I often asked myself "When would it be my turn?" I often dreamt that I was dying, and my parents tried to yank my feet, so I would return to them. I was frightened and felt totally lost.

I lost my will to live. I found a small knife next to my bed and was thinking of killing myself with it, but my brother found it and took it away. He was afraid that I really wished to end my life and he left his mobile phone with me, so I could amuse myself playing games. One day I threw it down with all my might and it was shattered.

One night when everyone was asleep, I tried to disconnect my ventilator, the machine that kept me alive. But once again, the doctor found me in time and they saved me.

Slowly I got better. However, I had to face the cruel reality that a wheelchair would be my friend for life. And it also meant that I had to give up my schooling. I imagined all the mocking and gossiping when people saw me. In my village, people believed that disabled people were ghosts of the forest in disguise. I remembered when I was at the orphanage I was very happy that their people loved and cared for me. But since I became ill, hardly anyone came to visit or even wrote to me and my future was a blur in front of me. I was at the so-called 'prime of life' and yet all I could see was darkness.

At that time, I would never have imagined that I would meet someone like Mother Tim. Hien, the social worker of Maison Chance, visited the hospital regularly and he explained to me that there were many people like me at Maison Chance. He described how they continued to live and work.

After that Mother Tim taught me how to live courageously. She told me never to give up when facing life obstacles. And yes, today I am still in a wheelchair, but I live among other members of Maison Chance. They are also like me, they have either suffered an accident or they were born unlucky.

Even now, I do not like to go out, except when I go to the market with my friend Que Nhung. I still feel the strange looks when people see me, so I don't go out.

My arms are still functioning, and I can continue going to school. Mother Tim always reminds me to do my best for the best results. When I am better physically and more mature, I can help others who are less fortunate. Therefore, I have started thinking about my future.

I went to Phu Quoc Island with all of the members of Maison Chance. Mother Tim carried me on her back and took me to the top of the highest mountain in Phu Quoc Island to look at the view. She emphasized that life is beautiful, and no matter what we would keep on living. So now I have no intention of ending my life.

I am learning to paint at the Take Wing Center. My first works were full of colors; I believe in my beautiful life. My aim is to continue my study and study more so that one day I am able to look after other orphans. That's my biggest dream and I know it will take a lot of money and effort to make it a reality, but I believe in love, the biggest motivation to get there. So now you all know my dreams.

# Le Quyen

*"Suppose one day your life was shattered by a horrendous event and its pain broke you up mentally and you wished to give up living. Then listen to me please, do not give up and keep moving forward, you will find a way. In life there is no dead end."*

My name is Le Quyen and I was born in 1988 in Khanh Hoa. I arrived at Maison Chance in 2012 and I have been here for the last five years. I turned a new page of my book of life when I arrived here.

If you had to begin again from the start, how would you feel? Was it easy? For me it was a very difficult task. To start again meant to change completely to accommodate my new life; the life of a useless paraplegic, depending always on the help of others. I led the life of a person who needed love and care but, at the same time, I was in fear of being pitied. What made me feel like that?

When I was 21 and a student at the University of Pedagogy of Nha Trang specializing in Early Childhood Education, I had a traffic accident. The doctor informed my family that "The operation will help your daughter, but she will have to use a wheelchair." To tell the truth I thought at that time I simply need a wheelchair temporarily and if I tried to exercise I could walk again. But after four months of hospitalization, I discovered that it was not true. It was obvious that I would have to be a lifelong wheelchair user.

After I was discharged from the hospital, I was desperately depressed. If it was you, what would you do? Would you listen to music? Watch movies? Read the newspaper? For me, I just sat in silence. I did not cry, and I only wished I could just walk for only one day. I watched my younger sister working always without a rest, even when she was not well. She still took care of me as I watched my parents working hard in the field under the scorching sun and yet I could not help in any way. I felt completely useless and selfish.

I realized that my pain was insignificant compare to the enormous hardship suffered by my family. Days passed, and I was bound to the wheelchair. Sometimes I was so pessimistic that my head was full of dark thoughts. Was this the end of my life? But at the same time my will to live emerged strongly and I needed to find a way to change my present circumstance. I told myself that I would not give up and I would find a way somehow.

I started searching by looking at YouTube on line, by reading newspapers, and by watching television. I searched for the important word 'disability', and then I found the link to 'Mother Tim and Maison Chance'. I searched further on the work of Maison Chance and tried to work out if this was the answer to my problem. I knew then that this would be my future.

I decided to speak to my mother about putting in an application to Maison Chance to be trained in some skills. My mother told me "You are not going anywhere, if you go there who will look after you? You stay here with us." To be truthful, at that time I was very frail. I could not take care of myself, so how could I even think of moving to Saigon to live on my own?

But I watched a lot more people who were even worse than me living and working at Maison Chance. I was stubborn by nature, so even if my mother objected to it, I still telephoned Maison Chance enquiring about an application. I talked to Uncle Hung, the concierge. He was enthusiastic and instructed me how to write an application.

With the help of my sister I wrote an application to send to Maison Chance. I waited for days and months for a reply, but none came. I found out from other disabled people that there were so many applications for a place at Maison Chance, maybe they had not even looked at mine yet. I was feeling a bit disappointed.

When I found out that Mother Tim had taken her children for a holiday to Nha Trang, I immediately called for a meeting with Mother Tim. I did not dare to open my mouth to my parents, but I asked my elder sister to take me to meet Mother Tim. I was feeling scared. What should I tell her? And how, my English was not that good?

But it turned out that Mother Tim was very easily approached and what a surprise to find out that Mother Tim speaks Vietnamese fluently. She talked to me like an old friend whom I had not seen for a long time. She then asked me if I would like to come home with her then. But I had not told my parents, so I asked for a week to prepare my leaving home.

At home, I talked to my father, showing him the images of the work done at Maison Chance. I said to my father that I would only stay for a couple of years to be trained in a skill and then I would return home. My father agreed and a week later I moved into Maison Chance. I was officially a member of the house.

At the beginning I found everything a bit strange. Watching the wheelchair riders as they rolled out on the road to go to work, I wondered if I would be able to do the same. The first time I went in my wheelchair from Maison Chance to the Take Wing Center, I found it extremely difficult and it was such a long way. But slowly the road seemed to be shorter. Everything began to be easier.

When I first arrived at Maison Chance I enrolled in Graphic Design and in October 2012 I moved to Village Chance working as an assistant kindergarten teacher. To upgrade my knowledge, I studied for six months at the University of Pedagogy in Saigon to receive a diploma in Kindergarten Management. I was studying Early Childhood Education before my accident, therefore Mother Tim suggested that I should keep on studying it and she constantly encouraged me to follow my dream. I decided to have a go with my new job.

I have now lived at Village Chance for five years and I have adapted my way of thinking to my new living environment. I have found a joy in my life. There are so many memories here; every morning together we got up, ate our breakfast and rolled our wheelchairs to The Take Wing Center to study. There were times we were caught in the rain, so we took shelter under a veranda and we chatted noisily. At the Center, listening to the happy laughter of the children strangely made me feel at ease spiritually. Their innocence was the motive for me to continue my earlier study and to work toward my future.

Thank you, father and mother. Thank you, Mother Tim and the other kind-hearted people. Thank you, all my friends at Maison Chance who are close to me and who help me to find the meaning of life.

Suppose one day your life was shattered by a horrendous event and its pain broke you up mentally and you wished to give up living. Then listen to me please, do not give up and keep moving forward, you will find a way. In life there is no dead end. I said so because every day when I woke up I still wondered what would have become of me if I did not search online for 'disability', and if I did not have the courage to contact and meet Mother Tim in Nha Trang.

Life always noiselessly hands out opportunities to us. Basically, we have to recognize them and grasp them on time. And that's what I think.

# Tran Quang Vuong

*"I often reminded myself that I should not think that the task is impossible until I have tried my best to do it and I should always try whenever I still can."*

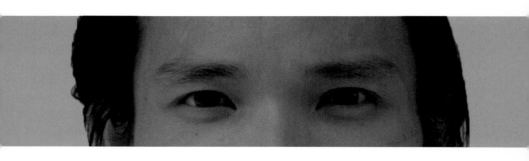

My name is Vuong and I was born in 1988 in Binh Thuan. I was the fifth child in a family of six. All year round we worked in the fields. My mother died when I was 12 and my father took over her job of taking care of us as well as working to keep us fed and clothed. We tried to keep up with our studies without my mother's care.

My life changed drastically when I was 11 due to an unpredicted event. During the school holiday in 2005, I had a casual job to help my family. One day when I was loading heavy goods onto the truck, I fell down and fainted. When I recovered I felt normal without any obvious pain, so I simply thought that I was just too tired when I fell and fainted. I did not seek any medical advice.

I continued with my normal life of studying and working, but six months later I started having pains in my back. I immediately went to see a doctor and he found that my spinal cord had been injured when I had my fall six months earlier. I was sent to the Orthopaedic Trauma Hospital in Ho Chi Minh City, where the x-ray and tests showed that my D-12 was damaged, so my family agreed for me to stay on at the hospital for further examination and treatment. A month later I was operated on to readjust my spinal cord. After recovery, I still experienced pain but I could still move my legs normally after the operation.

A month later I had to undergo a lumbar surgical implant which we thought would be the answer to my problem. However, the operation went terribly wrong and this changed my life permanently. Two days after the operation I woke up and I was in a panic finding that my legs were completely paralyzed. My family would not accept the fact that my future would be ruined so they tried many different treatments to save my legs. But after three months my family ran out of money and I did not make any improvement. They were utterly disappointed when the doctor informed them that I would spend my life in a wheelchair and he advised them to transfer me to the Saigon Rehabilitation Center in District Eight to be helped by physiotherapy.

I was admitted to the Rehabilitation Center for another three months for further treatment. Daily in the Physiotherapy Department I was taught to get in and out of the wheelchair as well as to care for my own personal hygiene and my own health. My physical health slowly improved but my legs were still completely paralyzed. At this time, my family was totally broke and they could not pay for me to stay on at the Rehabilitation Center, so they took me home.

At home, everyone had to work to repay all the debts incurred when I was in the hospital. My little sister, who was in year eight at school, had to look after me. Knowing that I would be a paraplegic for life, I was so depressed that I just wanted to kill myself. But when I thought of my family and my friends who cared for me, I had to stop being pessimistic.

One day when I revisited the Rehabilitation Center for my regular examination, the head nurse Miss Kim Cuong introduced me to Maison Chance.

By August 2007 I was accepted by Maison Chance and since then I have stopped having dark thoughts. I lived among the other members who suffered like me and yet they lived and worked happily. I started to be independent in my daily life and I went to physiotherapy every day to improve my physical health. After the treatment, I attended classes in painting, music and the French language.

In 2008, another calamity happened to me; the lumbar implant collapsed. I had to stop all my studies to be admitted into hospital for an operation to remove the implant. The surgeon managed to remove the implant successfully, but he could not replace it with a new implant when the wound was not completely healed.

I returned to Maison Chance without the implant and I ran into more trouble. Since the implant was removed, my damaged D-12 was getting worse. Maison Chance was looking for specialists in lumbar surgery in Vietnam without success since my case was quite unique with a main artery across the lumbar bone. If the artery was damaged during the operation it would be fatal. My chance of surviving was very small.

In 2014, Mother Tim raised enough funds to take me to France for an operation. In March 2014, I was taken to France, but my case was never simple. The doctor there realized that I had septicemia, therefore I had to have a complete blood transfusion before the operation.

On May 15, I underwent a successful eight-hour operation by the doctors in the City Hospital of Toulouse. Afterwards, I was transferred to the Roquetaillade Center at the Auch Commune for two months of rehabilitation. My wound healed, and my health was recovered.

I returned to Maison Chance in Vietnam on July 20, 2014 to continue my rehabilitation. I am much happier now and I love my life. I continue to exercise to improve my health and to attend my painting, music and French classes for a brighter future.

I often thought of becoming a painting teacher, but to obtain an official certificate from the University is beyond my capability. So, at the moment I am trying to broaden my skill in painting using a different medium, such as painting with sand to achieve a different style of work.

I was not born with a talent for painting like other painters, but I believe that success only derives from one percent talent while the other 99 percent depends on hard work and practice. I often reminded myself that I should not think that the task is impossible until I have tried my best to do it, and I should always try whenever I still can.

I can play the guitar. When I sing accompanied by the guitar all my pain and worries float away. In 2016, the precious stone carving room was established at the Take Wing Center and I enrolled in this class. I live an independent life at Village Chance. Though life has many challenges, I continue to live a useful life and I try to do my best, so I will not disappoint all those who care and love me.

# La Van Thanh

*"No matter who you are, if you have to face any difficulty in life, have faith that you will overcome it. Do not give up easily, do not say goodbye hastily to your precious life granted to you by the creator, hang on to it until your natural last breath."*

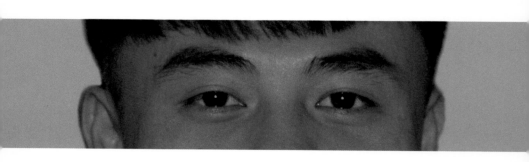

My name is la Van Thanh, I was born in Ho Chi Minh City in 1996. My childhood was not like another child's childhood. I was told my mother was a street walker, and my father was a drunk and a drug addict. People also told me that he abused my mother badly, and every day there was violent fight in my family.

I never knew what my mother looked like; she left me in the care of my father before I even turned one year old. I lived with my father and we never settled in anywhere for a long time; we moved constantly from one place to the next. I witnessed with my own eyes my father injecting himself with needle. He also tried to sell me to pay his debt, but I did not fetch a good price for him, so he did not sell me. I ended up living with another family who treated me badly; I had to do most of the chores in the house like a slave.

When I was nine I met a teacher, Mr. Thai, who felt sorry for my circumstances, so he took me home with him and sent me to school. He took care of me for three years, and then he arranged for me to move to Maison Chance.

At Maison Chance I was feeling the freedom of a fish in the water. We lived in harmony and we loved and took care of one another. We helped one another as if we were blood relatives. One day I received the news of my father's death; he died of cancer of the throat. I was devastated, even though he did not bring me up, but he was my only blood relative. I was in denial until I stood in front of his corpse of my father whom I had not seen for a long time. I did not recognize him at all; he was just skin and bones.

Bad luck did not come singly. On my 20th birthday I got the bad news from the doctor that I had contracted a serious illness and that I would not have a long time to live. It was a real bad day for me; the fever caused my body temperature to reach over 109 degrees Fahrenheit. I lost weight rapidly and I was covered with an itchy rash. I lost my appetite and often felt like vomiting. I was obsessed with dark thoughts and I was so sick of my ravaged body that I did not want to live any more. I was no longer who I used to be.

I was tortured with my sick body for months and when I had almost given up any hope, Mother Tim discovered my problem. She stayed by me, comforted me, fed me and made sure I took my medicine. I appreciated Mother Tim's love and care for me. Even though I was not her own son, she treated me as if I was. With the love and care of Mother Tim and my friends at Maison Chance, coupled with optimism and my belief in life, I slowly overcame my illness again. Even now I often thought how I managed to overcome all the obstacles.My physical health improved noticeable and so did my high spirits.

At Maison Chance I go to school every day. I work side by side with Mother Tim and my brothers and sisters. I just finished my year 12 of school and I am preparing for my university entrance. I want to specialize in Financial Management so when I graduate I can help to lighten Mother Tim's heavy workload. I have been living at Maison Chance for nearly nine years now. I have matured considerably, and I have learned to communicate, to relate to others and to think positively. These are the skills to give me self-confidence in life.

Although being a child without a family's loving care, without a fixed address and with a life filled with challenges, yet I managed to overcome them all. This accomplishment was mostly with the support of Maison Chance and the love of Mother Tim and partly with my own determination and optimism. I think this has been only a small trial, there will be more challenges awaiting me in future and I will have to overcome them before I can reach my goal. And to realize this I will need my will and my optimism.

People often say, 'After the rain, the sun shines brighter', the bright sunrays and the colors of the rainbow are not only the beauties of nature, but they also represent the rays of hope and the life source after the stormy dark times.

I wish to send to you, my friends, this message, "No matter who you are, if you have to face any difficulty in life, have faith that you will overcome it. Do not give up easily, do not say goodbye hastily to your precious life granted to you by the creator, hang on to it until your natural last breath."

We cannot save everyone, but we can help a lot of people to recover the balance of their lives.

I am very happy seeing most of the children of Maison Chance grew and matured and not only did they know how to take care of themselves, they are also aware of others in the community. They are truly admirable. They have the courage and energy to accept their unfortunate circumstances and to overcome them. They are a good example for me to follow and they are the people that I feel happy to offer my love and care.

The handicapped are not my blood brothers and sisters and the orphans are not my own birth children, but we are destined to meet and to live together as a normal happy family. LOVE IS A GIFT FROM THE GOD, WE GIVE IT AWAY AND IN RETURN WE RECEIVE BACK TWICE AS MUCH.

**- Tim Aline**

# Appendices

**Vietnam** occupies an area of 341,690 square kilometers (or approximately 131,927 square miles) with a population of 95 million in 2017. The names of the cities and provinces marked on the map are the places mentioned in this book

## CITIES

**❶** Ha Noi

**❷** Hue

**❸** Nha Trang

**❹** Gia Nghia

**❺** Đa Lat

**❻** Bao Loc

**❼** Phan Thiet

**❽** Vung Tau

**❾** Sai Gon

**❿** Phung Hiep

**⓫** Phu Quoc

_____

**⓬** Phnom Penh (**Campuchia**)

**⓭** Vientiane (**Laos**)

## PROVINCES

**⑭** Hai Duong

**⑮** Thanh Hoa

**⑯** Quang Ngai

**⑰** Kon Tum

**⑱** Gia Lai

**⑲** Đak Lak

**⑳** Đak Nong

**㉑** Binh Phuoc

**㉒** Lam Dong

**㉓** Binh Thuan

**㉔** Đong Nao

**㉕** Ben Tre

**㉖** Soc Trang

**㉗** Kien Giang

**㉘** Tay Ninh

## DISTRICT

**㉙** Krong No

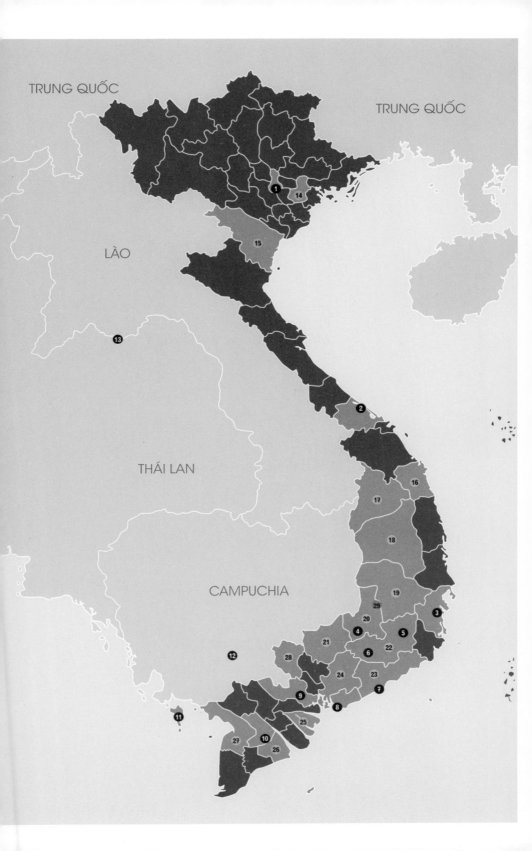

TRUNG QUỐC

TRUNG QUỐC

LÀO

THÁI LAN

CAMPUCHIA

# Information
# Maison Chance
# world wide

---

## Maison Chance Belgium

80 Albert Meunier Street

1160 Bruxelles, Belgium

Email; belgique@maison-chance.org

## Maison Chance Canada

5830 Canseau

St-Leonard, Quebec

H1P 1H9 Canada

Telephone: +1 514 955 8048

Email: canada@maison-chance.org

## Maison Chance USA

2503 - D N. Harrison Street #1128

Arlington, VA 22207

Email: usa@maison-chance.org

## www.maison-chance.org

---

### Maison Chance France

40 Domremont Street

75018 Paris France

Email: france@maison-chance.org

### Maison Chance Swiss

PO Box 5201

1003 Lausanne, Switzerland

Email: Suisse@maison-chance.org

### Maison Chance Vietnam

19 A Road No. 1 A, Quarter 9, Binh Hung Hoa A Ward

Tan Binh District, Ho Chi Minh City, Vietnam

Telephone: +84 (0)28 62 65 95 66/ 28 37 67 04 33

Email: vietnam@maison-chance.org

# MAISON CHANCE

*THE LUCKY HOUSE—A FUTURE FOR THE LESS LUCKY*

## Hoang Nu Ngoc Tim (Aline Rebeaud)

---

*Director of Publishing:* NGUYEN MINH NHUT
*Advisory Editor:* LE HOANG ANH
*Editor:* NGUYEN THI MINH TRANG
*Cover designer:* NGUYEN NGO THUY TIEN
*Layout artist:* VU THI PHUONG

---

TRE PUBLISHING HOUSE
· 161B Ly Chinh Thang, District 3, Ho Chi Minh City
Tel: (84.28) 39316289—39316211—39317849—38465596
Fax: (84.28) 38437450
Email: hopthubandoc@nxbtre.com.vn
Website: www.nxbtre.com.vn

TRE PUBLISHING HOUSE, HANOI BRANCH
No 21, A11 Dam Trau Quarter, Bach Dang Ward, Hai Ba Trung District, Ha Noi
Tel: (84.24) 37734544—35123395 Fax: (84.24) 35123395
Email: chinhanhhanoi@nxbtre.com.vn

TRE PUBLISHING HOUSE, DA NANG BRANCH
280D Trung Nu Vuong, Binh Thuan Ward, Hai Chau District, Da Nang
Tel: (84.23) 63539885
Email: chinhanhdanang@nxbtre.com.vn

YBOOK Co., LTD
A member of TRE PUBLISHING HOUSE
161B Ly Chinh Thang, District 3, Ho Chi Minh City
Tel: (84.28) 35261001 - Fax: (84.28) 38437450
Email: info@ybook.vn
Website: www.ybook.vn

---

Dimensions: 15 cm x 23.5 cm, National Standard Book Number 1518-2018/CXBIPH/6-88/Tre
Publication Control Number: 736/QĐA-NXBT, issued on July 10th 2018
Print run: 2.000 copies
Typeset, printed and bound in Vietnam by Southern Educational Promotion Printing Joint - Stock Company
Address: Block B5-8, D4 Street, Tan Phu Trung Industrial Park, Cu Chi, Ho Chi Minh City
Archived in the 3rd Quarter of 2018